Whither India in 2022?

BY THE SAME AUTHOR

Legends of Indian Cinema
Kokila: A Novel
Beyond Diplomatic Dilemmas
Modi's Midas Touch in Foreign Policy
Who Should Say Sorry for Two Millennia of Injustices?

Whither India in 2022?

Edited by

Amb. Surendra Kumar

HAR-ANAND PUBLICATIONS PVT LTD
E-49/3, Okhla Industrial Area, Phase-II, New Delhi-110020
Tel.: 41603490
E-mail: info@haranandbooks.com/haranand@rediffmail.com
Shop online at: www.haranandbooks.com

Published by Ashok Gosain and Ashish Gosain for
Har-Anand Publications Pvt Ltd

Printed in India at Aakash Press.

Preface

The book is a fascinating bouquet of essays by a dozen distinguished individuals from different walks of life who have shared their informed opinions about India at 75 years. They have not only taken a close look at the prevailing situation today but have also ventured to speculate where India is likely to be in 2022.

The Commerce and Industry Minister **Suresh Prabhu** is hopeful that by implementing PM Modi's Mantra: Reform, perform and Transform and continuing climbing up the ladder of Ease Of Doing Business, India's economy could become US$ 5 trillion economy in the next 7-8 years. The New Industrial policy envisages a globally competitive Indian industry of future equipped with skill, scale and technology focusing on 8 areas. Emphasis is on Start-up India which means producing job creators rather than job seekers and expanding scale of Production in 10 mission areas. There is an ambitious plan to take 12 Champion services of India to the world and increase India's exports of the agricultural produce to US$ 60 billion per year by 2022. India stands for globalisation and collaboration and opposes protectionism. GST and Bankruptcy and Insolvency Acts coupled with accelerated ease of doing business can lead to higher flow of FDI.

According to the MOS (IC) for Housing and Urban Affairs **Hardeep Singh Puri**, the architecture of the new urban development mission aims to meet challenges of growing urbanisation in sustainable manner, increase access to urban space and provide employment opportunities with devolution of power to the states and emphasis on innovative interventions and participation of the private sector. To fulfil the ambitious urban development vision, India has to boost its annual per capita urban capital spending eight fold from US$ 17 to US$ 135.

14 countries including the US, the UK, France, Canada, Japan, Spain and Singapore have been selected for city level Smart plan for 42 Smart cities. When implemented, SCM will benefit 32% of urban population; nearly 2855 projects have been proposed in 65 cities. Besides SCM, SBM, PMAY and HRIDAY will play a transformative role in sustainable urbanisation.

India needs an integrated urban policy consistent with the principle of cooperative federalism, inclusive urban development, universalisation of basic services and reduction of poverty. Municipalities and other local bodies have to be empowered to manage and maintain infrastructure services.

For the former governor **BP Singh**, maturing as a vibrant democracy with one person one vote, self sufficiency in food grains; changing initiatives like MNREGA and GST; efforts at providing equal opportunities to all and redressing educational and social deprivation and enhanced role played the Judiciary, Election commission, CAG and fiercely independent media have been unmistakable achievements of independent India. He feels that "the rise of India in the comity of nations is a tribute to its democracy and celebration of its diversity. Its achievements are based on political and economic liberty. However, India has a long distance to travel."

Governor BP Singh feels that India faces numerous challenges related to security, removal of poverty, generation of employment and effecting improvement in education, health care, corruption and criminalisation of politics. According to him," the criminalisation of the political process and the unholy nexus between politicians, civil servants and business houses is exerting a baneful influence on public policy formulation and governance." He goes on to say, "the more insidious threat to India's democratic governance is from criminals and musclemen who are entering the state legislatures and national parliament in sizeable numbers"

He stresses the need of embracing "Bahudha approach" and accepting the contrarian view and working for an inclusive India. He advises, "Development and secularism must go hand in hand"and "the govt, civil society organisations and market need to act in concert."

The former Chief Secretary of UP and Former Secretary General of the Rajya Sabha, **Yogendra Narain** draws attention to the fault lines of governance which he believes is a nebulous concept; it is much more than the sub total of the functioning of the parliament, the Executive, the Judiciary, administration, policy making and implementation etc. The politicisation of civil service, dent in the reputation of the judiciary and the sorry state of affairs in agriculture, education, health care and non-resolution of Naxal problem disappoint him.

Sushil Tripathi's paper on energy security takes an in-depth look at the energy sector as a whole underling the enormity of challenges in meeting India's growing energy needs in coming years. It also offers some sensible suggestions. In spite of India's current low per capita energy consumption (1/10 of the US, 1/6th of the European countries and 1/4th of China) India is the 3rd largest consumer of energy accounting for 5.5% of global energy consumption today. India's main challenges, according to Tripathi are: single fuel dominance and a disproportionate share of bio-mass in meeting energy needs. This is not likely to change significantly notwithstanding the ambitious target of 175 GW for renewable energy set by the govt. India's dependence on outside sources is evident by the fact that 80% of India's oil consumption, 50% of natural gas consumption and 15% of thermal coal consumption is imported. While coal would remain the main source of energy generation in coming decades, he feels that "gas could be one of the key sources of energy in India's energy mix as it could act as a transient fuel which will help India in achieving its energy accessibility targets with low carbon intensity."

He also opines that expansion of nuclear energy which presently accounts for only 3% of the total energy generation in India will help her meet both energy and environmental and emission goals.

Ideally India can emulate Japan, a net energy importer like her, which has achieved high level of economic and social progress without proportionate increase in energy consumption on account of efficient use of energy.

Mahendra Kumawat's essay is a dispassionate and objective commentary on several issues related to internal security: Kashmir,

North-East, Naxalism, terrorism, cyber crime, communal tensions and future wars for water. He also shares his views about communalisation of the police force, need of police reforms and training and recommends the creation of a new Interior Ministry.

He feels that militancy in the Kashmir Valley has evolved into insurgency which poses a formidable challenge to the state. According to him, "besides continuing security operations, the state need to work for winning hearts and minds of the people of Kashmir by granting greater autonomy, repeal of AFSPA from the areas where the army is not deployed and focusing on development at greater pace and good governance. He favours talks with Pakistan to convert the LoC into international border and to borrow a phrase used by former PM, Manmohan Singh, 'making borders irrelevant.'"

Taking note that Mizoram, Tripura and Sikkim have become free of insurgency but Assam, Arunachal Pradesh, Manipur, Meghalaya and Nagaland still face criminal activities of insurgent groups albeit much less than at any time, for a lasting solution, he recommends "rapid development coupled with emotional integration of the people of the Northeast with the mainland India."

He believes that, "so long as severe disparities in level of living, heavy incidence of unemployment, lack of economic opportunities, continued exploitation of disadvantaged segments of society and atrocities on the weaker sections, persist, the Naxal problem is not likely to be eradicated totally." An integrated yet multi-pronged strategy is the need of the hour. While coordinated and stringent security operations are necessary, simultaneous, imaginative and radical administrative, political and developmental measures are imperative to remove the Socio-economic malaise which has sustained the Naxal movement.

As for Terrorism, besides cross-border terrorism sponsored by Pakistan's Army and ISI ,now Islamic State is also striving to make its presence in India. So, he recommends the establishment of the 'National Counter Terrorism Centre' (NCTC) "to prevent terror attacks as the mandate of the NIA is only to investigate terror attacks once they have taken place."

Communal harmony, Kumawat maintains, has been frequently vitiated by political leaders who exploit communal tensions to garner votes. Regrettably India ranks at 4 place in the world after Iraq, Syria and Nigeria on account of social hostilities based on religion.

Mahendra draws attention to N.N. Vohra report which says that network of organised mafia in India is virtually running a parallel Govt.; this monster has gripped almost every aspect of national life.

He also underlines the need of investing in human resources, infrastructure and special training to address the threats posed by Cyber crime.

In Kumawat's view, SMART policing, augmentation of recruitment of police personnel, modern means of training and implimentation of various recommendations for police reforms are essential for meeting internal security challenges.

According to **Ajai Shankar** the grave air pollution situation in India is very grave; 14 out of 15 cities with highest air pollution in the world are in India. Our country has earned the avoidable distinction of having the highest death rate in the world from chronic respiratory diseases and asthma; air quality in Delhi reportedly damages lungs of 50% of children. Shankar feels that air pollution has become a national health crisis and ought to be addressed as a National Mission.

He advises subsidies on use of electric buses, large scale use of private electric cars, tax exemption to the owners of old cars to buy new cars and financial encouragement to farmers to plough back the crop residue in to the soil to convert it in to manure as some practical measures to bring down air pollution in the national capital.

He compliments India for having reached the installed capacity of 23000 MW of solar energy four years ahead of the deadline of 2022 and for having now set up an ambitious target of 100,000 MW by 2022. He hopes that with wider use of clean cooking gas more cow dung will be available for electricity generation in rural India.

Fund starved Municipal bodies can be helped by transfer of certain percentage of Swachh bharat cess and collection of GST for arranging treatment of Sewerage waste. Ajai is of the view that segregation of household solid waste, its treatment and compliance of prescribed norms for industrial effluents is a must for controlling pollution in cities/rivers.

He favours environmental audit, cluster by cluster, for assessing air, water and solid waste pollutants. But what's needed most for protecting environment to a great extent is the political commitment, process of consultation and consensus building, use of best talent and technology and affordability of required measures.

Chandrajit Banerjee has offered a very positive and forward looking perspective of India Inc. According to him, "India has displayed technological aptitude that is far ahead of its position as a middle-income economy. The country has achieved impressive milestones such as the 'Chandrayaan' mission to the moon, multi-satellite launches, R&D engagement, science and technology progress, internet and mobile phone connectivity, start up culture and other trends which place her within a huge window of exciting opportunity."

He refers to CII's India at 75 Vision which is an inclusionary process that aims at redrawing and achieving the vision for India. Guided by Late Prof. C. K. Prahalad, India@75 undertook a pan-India campaign to articulate a shared vision which embraced a wide spectrum of society including students, farmers, policymakers, housewives, slum dwellers and so on.

He Underlines the need of greater efforts at further improvement of education, health care, industry, employment and governance. According to Banerjee, "the task of strengthening India's inclusive development belongs to all sections of society, and industry has a special role to play in creating the new India," while "the government is playing a key role through a strong reforms process aimed at unleashing national entrepreneurship and easing the business environment."

Sounding optimistic, he adds "It is time for India to maximize the opportunities in a strategic and visionary mode. There is need to create a new template for growth, a new matrix of interconnectedness as a nation, a new definition of the nation's future. It is time for India to emerge as the fastest growing economy for the next three decades, to win the battle over poverty decisively, and to provide the best possible lives for people across the country, whether in tiny hamlets in remote places or in huge megapolises."

In **Prof. Chintamani Mahapara's** opinion, "the most significant development that altered the paradigm of India's engagement with the United States was the signing of the civil nuclear cooperation agreement."

During the Obama Administration's first term the US relations with India reached new heights exemplified by trade and investment, Joint Military exercises, defence trade, counter-terrorism cooperation, national security policy and the positive political chemistry between the Indian and American leadership. According to Prof. Mahapatra, "three key aspects of Indo-US relations under the Modi government and the Obama Administration were a broad consensus over building cooperation in handling Pakistan/ Afghanistan/terrorism conundrum; managing the muscular foreign policy of China and strengthening institutions and agencies that are part of defence and security matrix."

In spite of differences on a host of economic issues, including the visa fee issue, H1B visa issue, bilateral investment treaty negotiations and market opening issues Trump-Modi Administration have maintained good cooperation in Defence and technology trade and military to military relationship.

Mahapatra adds "One of the key developments in Indo-US relations under the Modi government and Trump Presidency is growing significance of the "Indo-Pacific" strategic concept ... instead of "Asia Rebalancing," the US would focus on peace, stability and development in the larger Indo-Pacific region. India has a prominent role to play in this strategic scheme."

However, India-US ties would be tested by developments in Afghanistan and along India-Pakistan borders. Mahapatra feels that India should carve out a place for itself in the loop that would unfold the future course of US action in Afghanistan.

Three million strong rich and influential Indian Diaspora would continue to serve as a strong bridge between the US and India; two Women of Indian origin namely Kamala Harris from California and

Tulsi Gabbard from Hawaii have already thrown their hats in the ring for the next Presidential race.

In Mahapatra's view, India's mantra of "strategic autonomy" has served her foreign policy well and facilitated her participation in two Trilateral: US, Japan, India and China, Russia and India. But she will have to do a smart tight rope walk in the US-China and US-Russia rift on a number of issues.

Mahapatra feels, while India's experiment with strategic autonomy is a goal worth seeking, in an interdependent world, the limits of "autonomy" need to be delimited. "And this is where the strategic thinkers and policy planners in India need to put their mind together" he adds.

Lt. General **Satish Nambiar** bluntly says that, "India's political leadership and civilian bureaucracy have been reluctant to recognize the contribution of its military to the making of the modern world and today's India."

He adds, "The unfortunate fall out of the political leadership's distrust of the military and its consequent exclusion from top level deliberations is that the civilian bureaucracy and the intelligence establishment have found it expedient to impose themselves between the military and the political leadership."

His views about the restructuring of the Defence ministry and advice that India should review her declared nuclear doctrine in so far as "No first Use" is concerned, might ruffle some feathers.

According to Brig. Gurmeet Kanwal, India's future wars will be fought under the nuclear shadow. Pakistan sponsored proxy war in Jammu and Kashmir and acts of terrorism in different parts of India, remnants of insurgencies in the North-East and Left Wing Extremism remain causes of concern and instability in the country. He adds that efforts at conflict resolution have so far produced mixed results.

He advises formulation of a comprehensive national security strategy, Military modernisation, up-gradation of combat capacities and significant enhancement of the defence budget. It's high time we have the Chief of the Defence Staff, he adds.

He recommends the rank of the MOS to the NSA and his deployment in the PMO. He feels, the NSA should have executive Power of oversight on both thc internal and external Intelligence agencies and should coordinate with the Min of External affairs, Min of Defence and the MHA

In his concluding article, Surendra Kumar applauds the message of Sabka Saath, Sabka Vikas, Chalein Saath Saath. In his opinion, "this idea is so all embracing; it can be adopted by the UN as one of its major goals! Without sincere and serious pursuit of this vision, it's impossible to achieve SDGs of the UN. In its underlying humanistic message, inspiring objective and the intrinsic values it espouses, it is as lofty as the concept of Vasudhiava Kutumbkam! If implemented in letter and spirit, it can transform India.

In nut shell, it encapsulates the philosophy of the Preamble of India's Constitution. It could be a guiding compass for good governance and addressing pressing domestic issues. If pursued with prudence, pragmatism and sensitivity, it can be equally effective and productive in conducting external relations, bilateral, regional and international.

This collection provides a lot of food for thought to those who wish to have a serious look at what we have achieved so far as a nation, and where we are heading to in coming years.

SURENDRA KUMAR

Contents

I

Commerce and Industry, Strengthening India's Foundation

– Suresh Prabhu

There is no debating that India is set to leapfrog economies world over in the next decade or less. Under the Hon'ble Prime Minister's vision of making India Great Again by 2022, India is trying to engage with traditional and new partners. India continues its push to remain one of the most open economies in the world, with its Gross Domestic Product (GDP) set to touch the USD five trillion mark in the next seven to eight years. Both manufacturing and service sectors are expected to grow at more than ten per cent in the immediate future, which creates opportunities for more inflow of Foreign Direct Investments (FDI). The new Ease of Doing Business (EODB) rankings also point towards an improving business ecosystem within the country and will aid India in continuing to be an attractive destination for FDI. Having said that, the growth which is achieved over the next four years will set the pace at which India achieves the ultimate heavyweight title.

In preparation of the impending bouts, the Ministry of Commerce and Industry of the Government of India has taken centre stage in perfecting the Indian economy's stance to achieve the ultimate goal of becoming the world champion. By doing so it is focussing on creating the perfect environment for boosting manufacturing and investments in India, and trade across borders. Following the Hon'ble Prime Minister's mantra of *Reform, Perform, Transform,* the Ministry has already initiated several new policies and reforms, and India is already looking to attract much greater investment and enhance its exports as it treads down the path of becoming a high-income economy.

A look into some of the key transformative policies by the Ministry impacting manufacturing, trade and investments, will highlight what to expect come 2022.

MAKING MANUFACTURING IN INDIA FUTURE READY–MAKE IN INDIA

Manufacturing growth in India has lagged in the recent past and in requiring a re look the Ministry is now focused at taking steps to ensure a spurt in economic activity within India. The focus is on facilitating forward and backward linkages within India and towards facilitating job creation across the value chain. A look into two major policies highlights the same.

The New Industrial Policy

After more than twenty-five years India is on the cusp of getting its new industrial policy. The new industrial policy envisages creating a globally competitive Indian Industry of the future equipped with skill, scale and technology, in other words creating a *Future Ready Indian Industry*. The policy will centre around three main themes, which are to prepare India for future industries; to modernize existing enterprises and infrastructure; and to equip the Indian industry with certain enablers.

With an eye on implementation and not just giving India yet another "plan," works are already underway to give face to the new policy. Implementation in India has often suffered owing to the lack of communication between various stakeholders—Centre and State governments, Industry, Academia etc.—resulting in inaction. Taking cognisance of that, the Ministry is driving two major initiatives. In the first, the path is being set for facilitating setting up of future industries. Road maps are being formulated under this initiative which will address not only policy issues but also infrastructure, research and development (R&D), and skilling issues across eight identified sectors of the future namely—Unmanned Arial Vehicles (UAVs), Genomics, Electric Storage, Active Pharmaceutical Ingredients, Advance Materials, Feedstock Chemicals, Robotics and Automation. The road maps will target to set up dedicated industrial parks to cater to these sectors with an anchor investor for each park grounded. To ensure seamless implementation sector specific task forces, with representation from all relevant stakeholders, have been formulated with the relevant ministries taking lead, with the Ministry moderating the interactions at the topmost level.

To further fast-track implementation at the ground level, the second initiative—District Level Development—will clearly define the role of the District Administration in economic development and empower it with the required strategic inputs to accelerate growth at the districts to ensure growth at the national level. This initiative will result in the creation of resource-based plans, for the District based on a bottom-up approach and implement them by ensuring that heads from all relevant stakeholders across levels work together through an empowered steering committee. District administrations will have a direct line to this committees to address any barriers to implementation.

With the focus on implementation the impending results of these two initiatives will showcase India's ability to surpass barriers. The cases germinating out of these focused initiatives are bound to boost the entire ecosystem to tap into the massive potential the India industry has to offer.

Focus on Increasing Entrepreneurial Activity—Startup India

With a focus on the Hon'ble Prime Minister's vison of *generating job creators over job seekers*, the Ministry has been promoting entrepreneurship through the Start up India campaign. The Ministry is clear on its role of facilitating entrepreneurs across the country, especially in Tier II and Tier III cities, through providing requisite platforms to propagate business ideas to the industry at large. The Ministry has been able to achieve main-streaming of entrepreneurs from across the country, more than two hundred thousand registered users leveraged the first of its kind online learning module (i.e. the Startup India Learning Program). The Ministry has also opened it doors to startups to make available their products and services on the Government e-Marketplace or GeM platform which aspires to become the Amazon of government procurement in India.

India is now house to one of the largest startup ecosystem in the world with over twenty thousand active startups. The Ministry has recognised close to seven thousand startups which have generated more than eighty thousand jobs pan India since the initiation of the campaign. Having said that, the Ministry is sensitised to the fact the journey ahead is a long one and has put in place a feedback mechanism to ensure that various policies relevant to the campaign are adjusted to the contemporary needs of the market.

INCREASING THE SCALE AND SCOPE OF INDIAN TRADE

For the first time in India's history, at least ten new missions are in the process of being set up with the mandate of growing India's export markets both in existing and new markets and products. The Ministry has also put into place an in-house state-of-the-art Trade Analytics Division to drive data-based actions. To be christened as the Market Development Missions of Indian Products, a multi-pronged approach will put in place to not only boost merchandise exports but also services exports which will rise even much faster. These missions will provide the channel for various initiatives being donned by the Ministry that will further push the growth in exports, which have been continuously growing in the recent past.

Taking Indian Services to the World

The Ministry mobilised the plan of focussing on further boosting the share of services in Indian exports. Twelve *Champion Services Sector* were identified—Information Technology and Information Technology Enabled Services, Tourism and Hospitality Services, Medical Value Travel, Transport and Logistics Services, Accounting and Finance Services, Audio Visual Services, Legal Services, Communication Services, Construction and Related Engineering

Services, Environmental Services, Financial Services and Education Services– against which a corpus of close to a billion US dollars has been approved. The Ministry is at the forefront of formulating action plans for each of these sectors to promote them domestically as well as globally. This will provide the required thrust to the services sector and will play a significant role in pushing the country's economic growth.

Taking Indian Agricultural Produce to the World

For the first time ever, a dedicated policy has been drafted to provide support to exports of agricultural produce. The National Agricultural Export Policy aims at reinvigorating the entire value chain from export-oriented farm production and processing to transportation, infrastructure and market access, by following the cluster-oriented development paradigm. The policy has been framed with a focus on export-oriented production and promotion, better farmer realization and seamless synchronization within the government.

The action-oriented policy aims at doubling the share of agricultural exports to over sixty billion US dollars by 2022 and become one of the top 10 exporting countries of agricultural products. In doing so, it focuses on boosting high value and value added agricultural exports, focusing on perishables, whilst also promoting novel indigenous, ethnic traditional and non-traditional categories. This will hold the key to achieving the Prime Minister's aim of doubling of farmers income by 2022.

Incentivising Export-Oriented Job Generation

Through the Foreign Trade Policy review a renewed focus was set on incentivising exports arising out of labour intensive sectors, especially from the micro, small and medium enterprises. The Ministry has increased the annual incentives two percentage points amounting to well over a billion US dollars. The beneficiaries of which include both merchandise and services exporter, with a special focus on the textile sector.

Rationalising Trade Through Standards

With an aim of ensuring that quality products both emanate out of India and enter India for the benefit of the Global and Indian consumer respectively, a complete revamp of the Standards and Compliance regime is underway. The Ministry is heading inter-ministerial consultations to chart out a framework of Standards definition, assessment and enforcement which will have a massive impact on not only enhancing India's export competitiveness but also rationalizing imports.

Taking Lead to Promote Collaboration in the Age of Increasing Protectionism

The Ministry has adopted a multi-pronged strategic approach to leverage multilateralism and bilateralism. Taking lead in the work towards countering the increasing level of protectionism a mini-Ministerial Meet for re-emphasising the tenets on which the World Trade Organisation was built was organized in India. For the first time ever, the Ministry signed a written declaration with the Chinese to ensure equitable access to markets on both sides with eyes set on the future to rationalising trade deficit in the immediate rather than cutting trade deficit.

ATTRACTING INVESTMENTS OF THE FUTURE

Shifting from Quantity of FDI to Quality of FDI

Over the recent past several sectoral caps under the FDI policy have been done away with, thereby resulting in record inflows of over sixty billion dollars into the country. Thereby making it the foremost investment destination in the world. With eyes on the future the focus has shifted towards achieving the right balance between the quantity of FDI and the quality of it.

The quality of FDI will be assessed by its ability to boost domestic manufacturing, create new jobs and value addition is sectors. The focus will be on industrialization beyond cities, at district levels.

National level surveys and impact dashboards will be created to collect detailed information, that will in turn allow policy makers to draw better insights as well as steer FDI into more relevant sectors.

Bolstering the Ease of Doing Business Across India

To attract greater investment and cross border trade, both the Centre and the States are working towards converting the ease of doing good business to the pleasure of doing business. India has already achieved the landmark of breaking into the top 100 in the World Bank's Ease of Doing Business indicators and is poised to improve this further and break into the top 50 countries. The ease of doing business eventually needs to be reflected across levels and efforts are being undertaken to eradicate various implementation barriers.

New ways of doing business is being promoted within the government; the Government e-Marketplace or GeM platform has already tapped into the power of seamless and transparent procurement of goods and services by using technology. GeM is now being used by several government entities and the specialised time comprising of private sector experts is pushing towards achieving a larger share for e-procurement.

Amongst many major steps being taken, work is underway to create an India Integrated Logistics Framework, which will leverage the One Nation One Tax regime brought in by the introduction of the Goods and Services Tax (GST). The framework will ensure seamless flow of goods and services with the country and abroad thereby enhancing the pleasure of doing business in India to levels never seen before. Work towards end-to-end digitization of all processes pertaining to trade is also underway.

CONCLUSION

The need for businesses, governments and citizens to work together has been propagated across the world in the 21 century. The World Economic Forum's System Initiative aimed at Shaping the Future has said that, in order to unlock the full potential of economic activity across the globe, there is a need to modernize trade and investment systems, enhance facilitation and be sensitive to the power of digital best practices. The Ministry has not put in place policies to fast track work under these broad themes but has gone a step ahead to strengthen the foundations which is bound to present India as a Champion Nation come 2022.

II

Urban India

*– Hardeep S. Puri**

Introduction

17 per cent of India lived in urban areas in 1951 when the total population was around 360 million.[1] Development economists very often describe India as a 'reluctant urbanizer.' The level of urbanisation in the country increased from 28 per cent in 2001 to 31 per cent in 2011[2] to partially corroborate this phenomenon. This proportion is small compared to China and Indonesia at 50 per cent, South Africa at 61per cent, 78 per cent in Mexico and 87 per cent in Brazil.[3] Continuing population growth and urbanization are projected to add 2.5 billion people to the world's urban population by 2050.[4] In some respects, urbanisation in India is *sui generis*. It is India's large population base that makes it so. The 40 percent of Indians who will live in urban areas by 2030 will comprise of 590 million because of the overall size of India's population.[5]

Urbanization is a necessary condition for economic growth as cities in India.

*Shri Puri is a Minister of State (I/C) for Housing and Urban Affairs.

[1]Census of India, 1951.

[2]Census of India, 2011.

[3]World Bank, data.worldbank.org.

[4]United Nations, World Urbanisation Prospects, 2014.

[5]Mckinsey Global Institute, 'India's Urban Awakening: Building inclusive cities, sustaining economic growth,' 2010, https://www.mckinsey.com/globalthemes/urbanization/urban-awakening-in-india.

generates 90 per cent of tax revenues and the majority of jobs with just a third of the country's population.[6] The 12th Five Year Plan stated that urbanisation is central to India's strategy of achieving faster and more inclusive growth because agglomeration and densification of economic activities in urban conglomerations stimulates economic efficiencies and provides more opportunities for earning livelihoods. Thus, urbanisation transforms the entire social milieu and increases avenues for entrepreneurship and employment compared to what is possible in dispersed rural areas. It, thereby, enables faster inclusion of more people in the process of economic growth.[7]

Economic growth increases demand for more infrastructure as infrastructure development in urban areas facilitates economic growth. In fact, India's growing economy has been placing high demands on power supply, roads, railways, ports, transportation systems, water supply and sanitation which need high investments. Compared to the demand, the total expenditure of the municipal sector accounts for about 0.6% of the national GDP, whereas it is substantially larger in comparable nations such as Poland (4.5%), Brazil (5%) and South Africa (6%).[8]

The GoI is committed to the Agenda 2030, including the Sustainable Development Goals (SDGs), as the country's national development goals such as "development with all, for all" for inclusive development and flagship programmes like Swachh Bharat Mission, Make in India, Skill India and Digital India, converge with SDG. NITI Aayog, the premier think tank for the GoI has been entrusted with the task of coordinating the SDGs. For this purpose, it has undertaken a mapping of the various schemes of the Government and identified supporting Ministries as they relate to

[6]The Global Commission, New Climate Economy Report, 2014-http://newclimateeconomy.report/2014/wp-content/uploads/sites/2/2015/02/NCE-case-study_india.pdf.

[7]Planning Commission, Twelfth Five Year Plan (2012-2017).

[8]Peterson, G. E. and P. C. Annez (2007); Financing Cities: Fiscal Responsibility and Urban Infrastructure in Brazil, China, India, Poland and South Africa. India: Sage Publications.

SDGs and their targets. A Government-wide approach has been adopted for sustainable development to emphasize on the cohesiveness of economic, social and environmental factors. Similarly, the respective States have been asked to undertake a similar exercise to map their schemes with the goals. Several State Governments have already initiated action on implementing SDGs. Further, the Ministry of Statistics and Programme Implementation (MoSPI) has been leading discussions for developing national indicators for SDGs.[9]

In light of the above discussion, this paper presents the financing requirements for urban infrastructure in India, discusses the progress of urban development missions and presents a futuristic perspective to inclusive growth of the nation. The Rakesh Mohan Committee (1996) constituted by the Government of India to estimate the funding requirements for urban infrastructure estimated infrastructure requirements up to 2005-06 based on annual GDP growth projections of 7.5 per cent during 1996-2001 and 8.5 per cent during 2001-2006. Infrastructure investment was projected to increase from 5.5 per cent of GDP in 1995-96 to 7.0 per cent by 2000-01 and 8.0 per cent by 2005-06.[10] The McKinsey Study (2010) on India's urbanization projected a capital investment need of US$ 1.2 trillion over the twenty year period 2011-2030 with the majority of capital spending in cities devoted to transportation and affordable housing.[11] At this rate, India has to boost its annual per capita urban capital spending eightfold from US$17 to US$134.[12] The Deepak Parekh High Level Committee on Financing Infrastructure had projected an investment of Rs. 51.46 lakh crore

[9]United Nations in India.

[10]Rakesh Mohan (2003). Infrastructure Development in India: Emerging Challenges. Paper presented in World Bank Annual Bank Conference on Development Economics, Bangalore, 2003. Retrieved from www.rakeshmohan.com/docs/ABCDE-infrastructure-Paper.doc.

[11]Mckinsey Global Institute, 'India's Urban Awakening: Building inclusive cities, sustaining economic growth,' 2010, https://www.mckinsey.com/global-themes/urbanization/urban-awakening-in-india

[12]*Ibid.*

(at constant 2011-12 prices) in infrastructure during the Twelfth Five Year Plan.[13] In 2012, the High Power Expert Committee (HPEC) on Indian Urban Infrastructure and Services, appointed by the erstwhile Ministry of Urban Development, Government of India had estimated investment for urban infrastructure over the 20-year period from 2012 to 2031 at Rs 39.2 lakh crore.[14] While the financial projections differ among various analysts, the crux is that financing needs are huge in the coming years and a large part of investment in the future has to compensate for the cumulative gaps in urban service delivery.

INITIATIVES TAKEN BY THE GOVERNMENT OF INDIA

Currently, the Government of India is working on redesigning the system architecture of Indian cities. Some landmark projects aimed at addressing urban development issues have already been taken up by the Indian government. Initiatives like Smart cities, AMRUT, Swachh Bharat and HRIDAY missions provide strategic entry points for foreign investment and a tremendous opportunity for partnership. The architecture of the new urban development missions is guided by the twin objectives of meeting the challenges of growing urbanization in the country in a sustainable manner as well as ensuring the benefits of urban development through increased access to urban spaces and enhanced employment opportunities. These missions work on the model of devolution of powers to the states.

The Government of India's interventions in the urban sector have been ongoing since independence. However, the urban sector received prominence in investment for urban infrastructure augmentation with the launch of the Jawaharlal Nehru National Urban Renewal Mission (JNNURM). The Mission launched in 2005-

[13]Deepak Parekh High Level Committee on Financing Infrastructure, http://planningcommission.gov.in/sectors/ppp_report/3.Reports%20of%20Committies%20&%20Task%20force/1.Second-Report-High-Level-Committee.pdf.

[14]High Power Expert Committee (HPEC) on Indian Urban Infrastructure and Services (2012) retrieved from http://icrier.org/pdf/FinalReport-hpec.pdf page 35.

06 was designed as a reform-linked investment mission to ensure financially sustainable development of the cities through efficient governance, better infrastructure and improved service delivery. The main thrust of this programme was to ensure improvement in urban governance so that the ULBs become financially sound with enhanced credit rating and ability to access capital markets for undertaking new projects.

NEW URBAN MISSIONS

Various flagship schemes have been launched, aiming to change the face of urban India with massive investments over the next few years. Missions are directed towards innovative interventions and inducing private sector participation in financing urban development in India. The involvement of the private sector in the creation and maintenance of urban infrastructure is expected to have a multiplier effect and attract more investment in the urban sector.

Smart Cities Mission (SCM)

The objective of the Smart Cities Mission is to promote cities that provide core infrastructure and give a decent quality of life to its citizens, a clean and sustainable environment and application of 'Smart' Solutions. The focus is on sustainable and inclusive development and the idea is to look at compact areas, create a replicable model, which will act like a lighthouse to other aspiring cities. The Smart Cities Mission is a bold, new initiative. This is for the first time that Ministry of Urban Development is using the 'Challenge' or competition method to select cities for funding and using a strategy of area-based development. This captures the spirit of 'competitive and cooperative federalism.' During the first round, 20 cities from 12 States were selected which included five capital cities. In subsequent rounds, 70 more cities were selected. Citizen engagement was one of the key aspects for the preparation of Smart City plans. The smart cities plans prepared involved the participation of about1.4 million citizens.

The SCM has generated as much interest abroad as in India. Global companies from a large number of foreign countries have participated in the bidding process for the selection. Companies from 14 countries—US, Canada, United Kingdom, France, the Netherlands, Spain, Italy, Belgium, Norway, Japan, Singapore, Hong Kong, South Africa and Abu Dhabi have been selected for the preparation of city level Smart City Plans for 42 smart cities. Ecorys Nederland BV of Netherlands prepared the Smart City Plan for Bhagalpur in Bihar. Tractebel Engineering SA of Belgium is associated with the Smart City Plan of Dharmashala in Himachal Pradesh. Haskoning DHV Consulting of Netherland is associated with the little known Dahod in Gujarat, Mott MacDonald of United Kingdom with Jaipur, Deloitte Touche Tohmastsu of Japan with Bidhannagar in West Bengal, and Data World of South Africa with remote Namchi in Sikkim are examples in this regard.

The SCM will benefit 32 per cent of the urban population. The total cost of the projects in 90 winning cities is Rs. 1,91,155 crore.[15] This includes pan-city solution projects to the tune of Rs. 36,306 crore and area based development projects amounting to Rs. 151,195 crore. Nearly 2855 projects have been proposed in 65 cities. Some of the notable sectors in which investment is proposed are—urban transport, area development (integrated planning, heritage management, etc.), smart solutions and energy. The GoI is providing a grant of Rs. 200 crore in the first year followed by Rs. 100 crore every year for the next three years. An equal amount on a matching basis will have to be contributed by the State/Urban Local Body (ULB). The central and state government funds will meet only a part of the projects cost. Balance funds are expected to be mobilized from borrowings from financial institutions as well as from the private sector. The central and the state share will contribute only 44 per cent of the total project cost. The cities plan to mobilise 20 per cent from PPP, 20 per cent from convergence, 3 per cent from loans and the remaining 13 per cent from other sources such as corporate social responsibility.

The SCM is being implemented by Special Purpose Vehicles (SPV) created by each city. State governments are expected to ensure

[15]https://smartnet.niua.org/smart-cities-network.

a steady supply of financial resources for the SPVs. The SPV will plan, appraise, approve, release funds, implement, manage, operate, monitor and evaluate the smart city development projects. The states/ULBs shall ensure that a dedicated and substantial revenue stream is made available to the SPV in order to make it self-sustainable and evolve their own credit worthiness for raising additional resources from the market.

Atal Mission for Rejuvenation and Urban Transformation (AMRUT)

AMRUT adopts a project approach to ensure basic infrastructure services relating to water supply, sewerage, septage management, storm water drains, transport and development of green spaces and parks with special provision for meeting the needs of children. Implementation of this Mission will be linked to promotion of urban reforms. Under this Mission, states get the flexibility of designing schemes based on the needs of identified cities and in their execution and monitoring. States will only submit State Annual Action Plans (SAAP) to the Centre for broad concurrence based on which funds will be released. The Ministry of Housing and Urban Affairs provides central assistance to the extent of 50 percent of project cost for cities with a population of up to 10 lakh and one-third of the project cost for those with a population of above 10 lakh. Central assistance will be released in three installments in the ratio of 20:40:40 based on achievement of milestones indicated in State Annual Action Plans (SAAP). Under the Mission, SAAP of Rs. 77,640 crore has been approved and 3,406 projects worth Rs. 55,695 crore are in various stages of implementation and 215 projects worth INR 15.7 crore have already been completed in the 500 cities in 36 States/UTs.

Swachh Bharat Mission (SBM)

The SBM aims at creating demand for sanitary services and infrastructure. The estimated cost of implementation of SBM (Urban) based on unit and per capita cost for its various component is Rs. 62,009 crore. The GoI share as per approved funding pattern amounts to Rs. 14,623 crore. In addition, a minimum additional amount equivalent to 25 per cent of GoI funding, amounting to Rs. 4,874 crore, shall be contributed by the States and ULBs.[16] The balance funds are proposed to be generated through various other sources, which include but are not limited to: private sector participation; additional resources from State government/ULBs; user charges; land leveraging; Swachh Bharat Kosh; corporate social responsibility; market borrowing and external assistance. The SBM involves construction of 10 million household toilets, 500,000 community and public toilets; and achieving 100 per cent scientific management of municipal waste spread over all statutory cities and towns in the country.[17] Until December, 2017, four million individual household toilets and 0.23 million community/public toilets were constructed. Nearly 51,734 municipal wards have door to door waste collection services and 1337 cities have been declared as open defecation free.[18]

Pradhan Mantri Awas Yojana (PMAY)

Pradhan Mantri Awas Yojana for provision of housing for all by 2022 was launched in June 2015. The programme provides central assistance to ULBs and other implementing agencies through states. The programme has 4 verticals: one is central sector scheme namely credit linked subsidy scheme, the other three are centrally sponsored schemes namely in-situ rehabilitation of existing slum dwellers using land as a resource through private participation, affordable housing in partnership and subsidy for beneficiary-led individual house construction/enhancement.

In the spirit of cooperative federalism, the mission has provided flexibility to states for choosing best options amongst four verticals of the mission to meet the demand of housing in their states. The process of project formulation and approval in accordance with

[16]http://www.swachhbharaturban.in:8080/sbm/content/writereaddata/SBM_Guideline.pdf.

[17]Gauba, R. (2017). Improving Urban Infrastructure. Indian Journal of Public Administration, 63(2), 165-175.

[18]http://www.swachhbharaturban.in/sbm/home/#/SBM(dashboard) retrieved on 7 December 2017.

mission guidelines has been left to the states, so that projects can be formulated, approved and implemented faster. The mission provides technical and financial support in accordance with the guidelines to the states. Such a housing approach has resulted in a record number of sanctioning more than 3.19 million houses since the launch of the mission. The construction has started for 1.69 million houses. Total 6,671 projects have been considered so far with an outlay of Rs. 1,72,294 crore involving central assistance to the tune of Rs. 49,537 crore.

Heritage City Development and Augmentation Yojana (HRIDAY)

HRIDAY seeks to preserve and revitalise the unique character of 12 heritage cities, *viz,* Ajmer, Amravati, Amritsar, Badami, Dwaraka, Gaya, Kanchipuram, Mathura, Puri, Vellankanni and Warangal. It facilitates inclusive heritage-linked urban development including water supply, sanitation, drainage, waste management, approach roads, footpaths, street lights, tourist conveniences, electricity wiring, landscaping, security, heritage revitalization, and livelihoods by exploring various avenues including involvement of the private sector. The duration of the mission is 2015-17. The Mission is a central sector scheme with 100 per cent funding coming from the Government of India. Cities are required to prepare Heritage Management Plans and develop DPRs for identified projects for availing assistance under the scheme. The Heritage Management Plans and DPRs can be developed by the National Mission Directorate and City Mission Directorates through SPVs/PSUs/State Para-statals/NGOs of repute. Funds are allocated to executing agencies on the recommendation of the Mission Directorate.

Further, in the context of growing demand for resources to finance ongoing urban infrastructure expansion, the Ministry of Urban Development has developed a policy framework for Value Capture Financing (VCF). This seeks to enable states and city governments raise resources by tapping a share of increase in value of land and other properties like buildings, resulting from public investments and policy initiatives, in the identified area of influence. Some different instruments of VCF are land value tax, fee for changing land use, betterment levy, development charges, transfer of development rights, premium on relaxation of floor space index and floor area ratio, vacant land tax, tax increment financing, zoning relaxation for land acquisition and land pooling system. The Annual Survey of India's City Systems 2015 also recommends that land utilization should be maximized to recover value for development and financing.

The infrastructure sector in India has evolved from purely government funded projects to newer business models involving partial or complete ownership of the private sector. The last decade has witnessed increased investments in the infrastructure sector, accompanied by more proactive participation from private sector in the form of Public-Private-Partnership projects, particularly in the road and power sectors. In order to attract the private sector, the Government is putting in place the appropriate regulatory and institutional frameworks. A Draft National PPP Policy, Model Concession Agreements for PPP Projects, and Model Bidding Documents for PPP Projects along with guidelines and manuals have been prepared to increase transparency and accountability. By the end of November 2017, 56 PPP projects worth Rs. 4,155 crore have started implementation across 22 Smart Cities and another 31 PPP projects worth Rs. 1,424 crore are at various stages of tendering process.

A FUTURE PERSPECTIVE

Given the huge scale of deficit in urban infrastructure, budgetary support alone cannot meet the huge infrastructure gap. This deficit can be overcome by involving private capital investment. GoI funds and the matching contribution by the states will meet only a part of the project cost. Additional resources have to be mobilized from other sources including collection of user fees, land monetization, borrowings from financial institutions, etc. Innovative financing mechanisms such as municipal bonds, pooled financing and convergence with other central government schemes and private sector participation have to be explored. Municipal bonds have a huge potential for fulfilling the massive investment requirement in the urban infrastructure sector. Apart from providing much needed term funding and promoting sound corporate governance standards in ULBs, municipal bonds are necessary for stimulating the revenue generation process of ULBs.[19]

A few challenges and tasks for the Government going ahead include putting in place an integrated urban policy consistent with the principle of co-operative federalism, promoting inclusive urban development with a mix of strategies that would consist of universalization of basic services including education and health; access to housing and putting in place a strategy for reducing poverty. Also, empowering municipalities and other local level institutions to manage and maintain infrastructure services would go a long way in improving urban India. The ULBs need to mobilise their own resources to become financially sustainable. Development of a robust urban information system would help informed decision-making, increased transparency and accountability that would help the country reach a new height by 2022.

[19]http://www.centreforambition.com/img/pdf/9.BackgrounderSeptember2016.pdf.

III

India and its Grammar of Democratic Governance

– B.P. Singh

INTRODUCTION

Democracy and governance mechanisms are not given constructs. They need to be worked out. This requires both patience and perseverance. There are several prerequisites which go to define grammar of democratic governance like the constitution and laws, political parties; leaders endowed with will to serve their people; competent civil service; professional police cadres; independent judicial courts; free media; and vigilant civil society among the many.

Seventy years ago a new era of freedom was ushered in India as a result of a long independence movement that actively began with the First War of Independence in 1857 and culminated in 1947. This nine decade period constitutes an epic period in India's ageless history. Soon after independence, India went to embark upon the ambitious path of democratic governance and to lay down rules of its conduct.

India's grammar of democratic governance in all its manifestations is a work in progress particularly when one sees that the United States started this journey 241 years ago in 1776. What is noteworthy is that the Indian people are marching on this path with confidence and determination.

The seven decade old story of India's democratic governance and its consequences need to be appreciated in the context of India's contemporary history; achievements of the last seven decades; continuing challenges; possibilities and future perspectives.

CONTEMPORARY HISTORY

Quit India Movement and Azad Hind Fauj.

In our contemporary history three events stand out: (i) Quit India Movement and Azad Hind Fauj; (ii) Partition; and (iii) framing of the Constitution of India.

The 'Quit India Movement' was an important milestone in the India freedom movement. It was this movement that galvanized the entire nation to work for attainment of freedom from the British Rule. Mahatma Gandhi had expressed that, "Let the British leave India either to God or to anarchy." Consequently, the Congress Working Committee on 14 July 1942 approved a resolution declaring that the immediate end of British rule in India was an urgent necessity. Subsequently, the All India Congress Committee met on 08 August 1942 in Bombay, and endorsed the Quit India Resolution by an overwhelming majority. It also sanctioned starting of non-violent mass struggle. In an inspiring public speech, Gandhi ji told the people to'do or die' for the cause of freedom. On 09 August 1942 Gandhi ji and prominent leaders were arrested. The British Indian Government declared the Congress unlawful and sealed and seized its offices. The people retaliated by attacking police stations, post offices, snapping telegraph wires, uprooting railway tracks and blowing up bridges. The colonial government went about ruthlessly suppressing the people's movement. The movement, however, gained momentum everywhere.

Side by side in 1942, the Azad Hind Fauj or the Indian national Army (INA) was formed in Singapore. At the urging of their Japanese captors, almost 20,000 Indian prisoners-of-war had come together to form this army with the air of freeing India from the British rule. Netaji Subhas Chandra Bose provided the charismatic leadership. In October 1943, Netaji proclaimed at Cathay Building

(Singapore) the formation of the Provincial Government of "Azad Hind" (Free India).

PARTITION

On 15 August 1947, India attained freedom but it was an India divided into India and Pakistan. The British proposal to 'cut and quit' India was an elite project of the British administrators and their political masters as well as leaders of the Muslim League. The partition was accepted by the Congress Party after some initial opposition. The British withdrew hastily. Winston Churchill, no friend of Indian independence, termed it as a "*shameful flight.*" This partition was accompanied by unprecedented violence with one million dead. It created more than 11 million refugees. This was followed by Pakistani attempt to capture the state of Jammu and Kashmir forcibly. Pakistan continues to be in control of a large tract of the State (POK). Finally in 1971 Pakistan lost control over its eastern half known before partition as East Bengal, which is now Bangladesh. The civil war that resulted in creation of Bangladesh witnessed the Pakistani army killing over half a million of its fellow Muslim citizens in the east. There are a number of territorial disputes with and cross-border terrorism emanating from Pakistan. These continue to make impact on other neighbouring countries particularly Afghanistan and China.

Partition, a decision taken in haste by a handful of men, has proved a monumental failure. The people of the region, where millions are still living below poverty line are in dire need of improvement in their economic conditions. Was the partition of India merely a division of one Nation into two? Or the breaking of a civilisational ethos that held good for centuries? How long would the youth of the region tolerate it under the fear of vested interests and the radical mullahs?

I have always viewed that Partition was both a political failure as well as a civilisational one. Should the youth of South Asia not ponder over their contemporary history and focus on how they might co-operate in building a better future?

The Partition created unprecedented crisis and continues to do so. In particular the Partition raised mind-walls and spread hatred. Today, the situation in India's neighbourhood is not conductive to peace as Pakistan not only provides safe havens to terrorist outfits but uses terrorism as an instrument of state policy. All these are directly related to Partition. The Pakistan Army, the Mullahs among others have developed vested interests to persist with these divides. It has caused armed conflicts between India and Pakistan (in 1947, 1965, 1971 and 1999). In 1971 Pakistan was divided into Pakistan and Bangladesh on ground of language. The inept and callous military and political leadership accelerated the process.

Thankfully a new wind has started blowing in the 21 century. People are looking at their past afresh and entertaining new ambitions fuelled by forces generated by information technology and, from movement of capital and technology. Would globalisation and its twin sisters: technology and capital supported by new innovations in education, create a new set of social relations, and a fresh approach towards unity and harmony in society, polity and economy in South Asia? Would the new elite of India, Bangladesh and Pakistan overcome the partition crisis in the 21 century? However, this is a matter of future. I am hopeful.

CONSTITUTION AND SETTING OF NATIONAL GOALS

The Constituent Assembly of India consisting of 389 well known leaders of India worked tirelessly to frame the Constitution. They devoted 2 years 11 months and 18 days of extremely hard work in the making of the constitution of India. Dr. Rajendra Prasad (1884-1963) was the President of the Constituent Assembly. Dr. B. R. Ambedkar (1891-1956) played a pioneering role in the Assembly. His contribution went a long way in securing universal adult franchise rising above considerations of religion, ethnicity, caste and gender and in giving content to this fine document which, in turn, has been guiding the Republic in changing times.

ADOPTION OF NATIONAL GOALS

It was against this backdrop that the members of the Constituent Assembly of India adopted a pledge on 14 August 1947, which resolved "*At this solemn moment when the people of India through suffering and sacrifice, have secured freedom and become masters of their own destiny, I, a member of the Constituent Assembly of India, do dedicate myself in all humility to the service of India and her people to the end that this ancient land attain her rightful and honoured place in the world and make her full and willing contribution to the promotion of world peace and the welfare of mankind.*" On 14 August 1947, Jawaharlal Nehru in his famous "**Tryst with Destiny**" speech in Central Hall of Parliament declared: '*Long years ago we made a tryst with destiny, and now the time comes when we shall redeem our pledge.*' He reminded the country that the task ahead included' *the ending of poverty and ignorance and disease and inequality of opportunity.*'

CONTEXT AND PERSONAL BACKGROUND

How should one try to understand and explain 70 years of democratic India–a country of antiquity and enormously rich civilisation spanning over five millennia? The uniqueness of India and dynamics of its society and polity make it difficult to capture nuances of various facets of development and its consequences. The assignment becomes more difficult for a person who was born in 1942 in a family of freedom fighters and who has been an active participant in the governance of the country, in formulation as well as implementation of plans and programmes at district, state and national levels. And yet in all humility I accepted this daunting task.

I became Culture Secretary to Government of India in 1995 and one of my important duties was to organise the Golden Jubilee Celebrations of India's Independence on 15 August 1997 in the Central Hall of Parliament, in the States and in major centres of the world through our missions abroad.

Two incidents are worth mentioning. First, we issued an advertisement requesting citizens of India to share their thoughts on the occasion. Nearly two million responses poured in which were then evaluated and reply (unsigned) was sent to each person. Second, 15,000 freedom fighters were invited to witness the ceremony at India Gate and to participate in the march to Parliament to be led by Prime Minister Inder Kumar Gujral. At the midnight ceremony in the Central Hall of Parliament, recorded speeches of our freedom leaders i.e. Mahatma Gandhi, Jawaharlal Nehru, and Netaji Subhas Chandra Bose were relayed. At Vijay Chowk, one freedom fighter exclaimed that it gave him joy similar to "getting married again"!! Another freedom fighter came all the way from Allahabad to compliment me for broadcasting Netaji's speech as this was done for the first time from Central Hall of Parliament. The written responses to our advertisement were full of expressions of enormous satisfaction that we are a democratic country but several of them reminded us of the urgency to "*redeem the pledge.*" They highlighted that national leaders during the freedom struggle and in early years of the Republic, had repeatedly assured the people of securing for all citizens: equality, dignity, security, justice and employment. But they remain to be fulfilled.

Have we *redeemed the pledge*? The Constitution of India in the making of which B. R. Ambedkar bestowed visionary leadership as Chairman of its Drafting Committee was adopted on 26 January 1950. The Constitution has given us a magnificent structure to build the idea of India through democracy and its institutions. We have moved on this path relentlessly and several achievements are to our credit. There are many unfinished tasks to be accomplished and several shortcomings and lacunae in our system and finding new ways of working it need to be attended to.

ACHIEVEMENTS

India was once a flourishing civilization and a prized destination for trade and commerce that set Christopher Columbus on a discovery voyage. Between Columbus failed discovery of India in 1492 and India's Independence from the British in 1947, India had been robbed of her prosperity and left in a state of utter penury.

Since 1947, we have made rapid strides. For example, in 1947, more than three quarters of all Indians lived in poverty. Today, less than a quarter of them live in poverty. Nearly half a billion Indians have been lifted out of poverty in the last seven decades, a feat that has few parallels. In 1947, more that 80% of Indians were illiterate. Today, just 25% of Indians are. Our achievements are many. **Four** of these are required to be specifically highlighted.

First, India went on to establish popular sovereignty, which meant rule by the people through their freely elected representatives. It was for the first time in recorded history that India established a democratic system of government and polity management (notwithstanding some experimentation in democracy in Vaishali in Bihar and in Buddhist Sanghas in the past). Today India is not only the largest democracy in the world but also the most vibrant one.

A bold and magnificent decision was taken to introduce the system of *one person, one vote and one vote, one value* in the country. The universal suffrage paid rich dividends and the subsequent devolution of power to grassroots levels has helped consolidate the gains. Democracy is at the heart of governance in India.

The establishment of democracy in India challenged the traditional view of many thinkers, especially in the West, that democracy must have some a priori conditions like economic development, high levels of literacy and a common language. In fact Indian democracy has blossomed in the midst of poverty, illiteracy, and diversity. It must be said to the credit of the Indian people and their freedom leaders that they not only established democracy in a plural and poor society, but also made it successful and stable, vibrant and result- oriented.

A striking feature of Indian democracy is that elections are held at regular intervals in a free and fair manner based on universal suffrage as also the transfer of power from one political party or coalition to another takes place in a routine fashion. The electoral processes in India are fairly simple and well understood by the people. It is no surprise that democracy has become the institutionalized expression of the strength of the Indian electorate.

Another favourable feature in India is the increased participation of the common people in politics. Discussions of politics in urban as well as in rural areas are on the rise. People value their political rights and opportunities and exercise their votes in the elections to Panchayats, State Assemblies, and the Lok Sabha regularly.

The most remarkable achievement of Indian democracy has been to unify the country and in this Sardar Patel played a historic role by securing merger of 565 princely states in the Indian Union in a short time. Since then we have been able to keep the country united and its institutions of democracy functioning. This is particularly impressive in the context of partition of India which resulted in killing of more than a million people and displacement of millions of others. The architecture of constitutional democracy has prevented extremist organizations from wrecking the ship of the Indian State.

Second, the Indian democratic system introduced economic content in polity management. One of the significant triumphs of this approach is that India is self-sufficient in food production notwithstanding huge growth in population since 1947. Adoption of imaginative policies has also ensured that food is available to every citizen of our country thanks to programs like food at lower price for persons below poverty line and employment under schemes like MNREGA, and a common market and supported by an all India banking system. The adoption of Goods and Services Tax (GST) regime is an important landmark in this behalf.

India's political leadership, policy makers, and business brains are motivated by a strong desire to make the country a major economic power in the 21 century. The high rate of economic growth coupled with comfortable foreign exchange reserves and rising Sensex figures have imparted in them a growing confidence. India is aiming to have a high growth rate with a focus on equity. Although these two objectives are not always contradictory, conflict arises when scarce resources are diverted to meet the demands of the growing middle class or business houses by ignoring the requirements of the poor and the underprivileged.

Third, our Constitution is committed to two different sets of principles that have a decisive bearing on equality. First, is the principle of equal opportunity for all and the second, the principle of redressal of educational and social deprivation. Our preferential policies in government employment were initially confined to persons belonging to Scheduled Castes and Scheduled Tribes. After the acceptance of the Mandal Commission Report by the Government of India in 1990, reservations were extended to candidates from other notified backward classes as well.

One of the advantages of affirmative action has been an improvement in the distribution of opportunities among the Dalit's and backward classes. Ordinarily, children of poor and lower status parents get lower level jobs, and consequently, lower salaries and income. The reservation of jobs at all levels has ensured that the children of Dalit's and backward class parents are selected for all-India Services like the IAS and the IPS. The advantage, however, has not as yet percolated to the entire community of poorer and lower status parents.

In the scheme of affirmative action that the Constitution offers, the State has been authorized to make special provision not only for the advancement of socially and educationally backward classes of citizens, for the Scheduled Castes and the Scheduled Tribes, but also for women and children. Significant measures have been taken in this regard during the last seventy years. One such step relates to reservation of seats for women in local bodies. More needs to be done.

We are living in a period of time in which, encouraged by affirmative action incorporated into the Constitution about Scheduled Castes, Scheduled Tribes and Other Backward Classes, several communities are demanding similar entitlements. One has not only witnessed protests, but at times violent conflicts in the streets on the part of some communities demanding reservation. All these constitutional steps of empowerment are within a framework, which itself now demands re-examination and corrective measures so that the fruits of affirmative action reach those who must have them. The moot question is not only of the extent to which reservation in Government employment has really changed things for the better, but also how it could benefit, in particular, the marginalised sections of the backward classes as benefits of reservation are getting monopolised by families which are well to-do families belonging to this class.

Fourth, Several public institutions of Indian democracy like the judiciary, the Election Commission, the audit system, the media, and some public bodies built over the decades are strengthening the processes of democratic functions in an admirable fashion. The Right to Information given to the people is another step that has empowered them.

Is the stability and success of Indian democracy a sui-generis phenomenon reflecting the plural character and age-old values of Indian culture and heritage? Could it be ascribed to the calibre of India's freedom leaders? Is this solely due to the Constitution that India has? Was this success on account of the leaders of the Indian government as well as of states? In my view, all these factors have contributed to both the stability and success of Indian democracy. In fact the civilizational strength of India, that has over the millennia accorded tolerance and given consideration to different points of view, provided fertile ground for democratic institutions to take root.

The rise of India in the comity of nations is a tribute to its democracy and its celebration of diversity. Its achievements are based on political and economic liberty. However, India has a long distance to travel.

CONTINUING CHALLENGES

The Indian political economy is facing manifold challenges. These primarily relate to security and justice; removal of poverty; generation of employment; effecting improvement in education and health care; and corruption and criminalisation of politics.

SECURITY AND JUSTICE

The primary responsibility of the state is to provide security of life and property to every citizen.

The Indian State is facing a serious challenge to its authority from lawless elements. The Jihadi terrorism in Jammu and Kashmir and its ad hoc but frequent spread to other parts of India; the insurgency in the North-East; and the rapidly expanding base of the Naxalite movement in mainland India constitute grave challenges to democratic governance. Fortunately, one sees national consensus against Jihadi terrorism and it is for the Indian state to deal firmly with this menace. Insurgency in India's North-East is largely confined now to Nagaland, Manipur, and Assam and these are being tackled by democratically-elected state governments with full support from the Centre. The Naxalite movement which is widespread in India's heartland is popular among the rural poor and indigenous tribes. The Naxalites have embraced the Maoist ideology which is opposed to democratic governance and the constitution of India. They believe in violence and forcible capture of political power. Naxalite menace has been controlled affectively at some places when the state system acted with imagination and resoluteness. It is essential to deal with the problem effectively in a co-ordinated fashion duly supported and guided by the leadership of the state and at the centre.

Access to justice entails that a citizen knows his rights as well as the forum where he can seek redress. In reality there are many citizens who do not know their rights, or cannot afford to fight and do not even know where to get help. Another challenge for such citizens is the complexity of legal proceedings themselves, apart from their length and cost. For example, at the end of 2016, over 28 million cases were pending in high courts and subordinate courts in the country. Systemic solutions are, therefore, called for strengthening access to justice. At the same time, ad-hoc measures are required to give immediate assistance to the needy citizens.

REMOVAL OF POVERTY

During the last 70 years millions of people have been lifted from poverty level and have joined the middle class. And yet nearly 200 million out of 1.3 billion people remain below the poverty line in the country. There is a high concentration of persons below the poverty line in the large and poorer states of the north and the east. It is imperative to correctly identify persons below the poverty line and computerise the list. It would be possible then to give them economic advantages directly. This economic criterion will naturally cut across religion and caste lines, rich and poor states, and also across rural and urban areas.

If India succeeds in giving its youth quality education and skills, democratic governance will be greatly strengthened. Today, the youth has a choice between world-class engineering colleges and joining Naxalite camps and criminal groups. The Naxalite option needs to be effectively closed and criminals brought to justice.

Can India's democracy rise up to tackle these critical issues? These include: effecting improvement of service delivery systems; accommodating the dispossessed and marginal communities within policy making systems; and imparting skills to the marginalized so that they may become beneficiaries of the market mechanism.

EMPLOYMENT

The most challenging task facing India's political economy is the generation of gainful employment for the youth. India has more than 800 million people in the working age group of 18-35 years, the largest in the world. Every month, a million young boys and girls become eligible to join the work force. The availability of jobs despite rapid economic growth has not kept pace with the rising number of job aspirants—a phenomenon which some commentators call 'jobless growth'.The situation is going to be complicated by induction of new technologies in manufacturing and services sector. The large size of 'technologically unemployable youth' particularly in states in the north and the east will add to the enormity of the problem.

A mechanistic view of growth assumes that demography is destiny. But this by itself does not add to prosperity, unless young people are educated and skilled and new jobs are created. If we fail to equip the youth with good quality education and skills, India's demographic dividend could become a serious challenge to stability of the polity.

EDUCATION AND HEALTH

45. Besides employment to the youth, India has to rapidly work for providing quality education to children and healthcare facilities to all. In addition, the state has to pay particular attention in provisioning of health care facilities to working people, the elderly, the children, the sick and the poor. The public spending on health and education, however, is typically enjoyed more by the well-to-do. The schools and health centres in areas where the poor live are often dysfunctional and extremely low in quality.

Many studies have shown that the children in India have the necessary intelligence and potential but they should have access to quality primary and secondary schools. Unfortunately, most of our government schools are not functioning properly. Teacher vacancies and teacher absenteeism continue to plague these schools. As a result half of ten year old students of government schools cannot read a paragraph meant for seven year olds. Many teachers are simply not up to the job. Curriculums are overambitious. To make the system more meritocratic and accountable, teachers should be recruited for their talents and not their political connections. The situation is slightly better in private schools but they are very expensive and are invariably not located in rural areas.

It may be recalled that for centuries India had excellent centres of learning both at school and higher education levels. This contributed immensely in the making of India civilization as one of the most glorious in the world. Today, the country badly needs to strengthen its higher learning centres to facilitate innovations in important areas of human knowledge.

The health care facilities in the country too are in disarray. The situation is worse in several states and particularly in rural areas where seventy per cent of the population lives. It is true that cities have numerous private hospitals and clinics and have better doctors and the services. There is requirement to improve primary health care centres in rural areas. This could be done by building clinics in rural areas and developing streamlined health IT systems. The need for skilled medical graduates and nurses is rapidly growing in the country and it must be urgently addressed.

Fortunately the Government of India have taken steps to formulate new Education policy and Health policy. These need to be adopted and implemented in view of their importance. In fact, this constitutes a major challenge to the Indian state and is required to be attended to with promptitude. An imaginatively crafted monitoring mechanism would be of enormous assistance to ensure quality delivery of services to people.

CORRUPTION AND CRIMINALISATION OF POLITICS

The criminalisation of the political process and the unholy nexus between politicians, civil servants, and business houses is exerting a baneful influence on public policy formulation and governance.

The more insidious threat to India's democratic governance is from criminals and musclemen who are entering into State Legislative Assemblies and the national Parliament in sizeable numbers. A political culture seems to be taking root in which membership of state legislatures and Parliament is viewed as a means for seeking private gain and for making money. The Gandhian values of simple living and selfless service to public causes are rapidly vanishing. The rule of law at times is sought to be replaced by the rule of men. The Election Commission and Parliament are concerned with this problem. It is imperative that a more stringent legal regime is adopted and put into operation urgently.

The high level of corruption in India has been widely perceived as a major obstacle in improving the quality of governance and as an impediment to inclusive growth. While human greed is obviously a driver of corruption, it is the structural incentives and poor enforcement system for punishing the guilty that have contributed to the rising incidence of graft in India. The complex and non-transparent system of command and control, monopoly of the government as a service provider; underdeveloped legal framework, lack of information, and weak notion of citizens' rights have all given incentives for corruption in India. We have to adopt a more effective system that punishes the guilty with speed and protects the reputation and honour of honest citizens including civil servants, business entrepreneurs and politicians.

POSSIBILITIES AND FUTURE PERSPECTIVES

There are enormous possibilities of India strengthening itself in economic, military and cultural terms in coming decades. The rise of India is getting noticed in every sphere of human activity ranging from sports to space, computer software to pharmaceuticals, yoga to dance forms. The path of progress and development, however, is not easy in view of India's neighbourhood and social challenges within. We cannot afford to indulge in foreign policy adventures nor ignore the demands of disadvantaged groups for more avenues in employment, education and healthcare. Simultaneously, we have to strengthen our military and strategic capabilities.

In terms of India's goal of making "full and willing constitution of the promotion of world peace and the welfare of mankind," India has consistently given full support to the UN peace keeping efforts and continues to do so. India also decided to take an independent stand between the two super-powers i.e. the United States and the Soviet Union, and provided leadership to the non-aligned movement. However, India gradually tilted towards the Soviet Union. In today's unipolar world, India has moved towards the United States.

It may be mentioned that during China's India War in 1962, at India's request, the United States provided military aid and there was close cooperation between the two countries on intelligence issues. By 1968 most of those links were gone.

The National Security Strategy (NSS) document of 2017 of the United States, the Trump administration has declared that "*We welcome India's emergence as a leading global power and stronger strategic and defence partner,*" on to say: "*We will expand our defence and security cooperation with India, as a major Defence Partner of the US... We will deepen our strategic partnership with India and support its leadership role in India Ocean security and throughout the broader region.*" India has welcomed the US move. The Foreign ministry said that, "close partnership between India and the US contributes to peace, stability and prosperity in the indo-Pacific region as well as to the economic progress of the two countries." Appreciating the "strategic importance given the India-US relationship," it further said, "India and the US share common objectives, including combating terrorism and promoting peace and security throughout the world."

One of the lessons of Indian history is that we have suffered in numerous ways on account of weak government at the centre and in absence of strong military. One has to keep these constantly in view in coming decades of the 21 century as well. Ramdhari Singh Dinkar puts it beautifully when he writes:

क्षमा शोभती उस भुजंग को,
जिसके पास गरल हो।
उसको क्या, जो दन्तहीन,
विषरहित, विनीत, सरल हो?

Mercy is becoming of that dragon,
Who possesses the poisonous fangs.
The one toothless, with no venom in bite,
Though humble, simple, is of no consequence.

History is moving fast in terms of demography, culture, urbanisation, and expansion of human consciousness. All these changes accompanied by a phenomenal rise in expectations would pose unforeseen challenges. The Indian leadership is required to make policy choices in several economic, social, cultural, and external arenas in order that we can successfully synergise our strengths and abilities for technological innovation, problem solving skills, and political vision. India's elite in politics, the media, the academia, and think tanks have the capacity to re-define the issues and recast the public debate.

Mahatma Gandhi wanted all of us to *work for an India in which the poorest shall feel that it is their country in whose making they have an effective voice; an India in which there shall be no high class and low class of people; an India in which all communities shall live in perfect harmony.*

Democracy is increasingly defining new features of development and governance. Democracy during the last seven decades has gone beyond periodic elections towards good governance and participation of stakeholders in development programmes.

The building of an inclusive society requires deep understanding of social, cultural and economic forces, hard work and tenaciousness. The crucial task is to empower the marginalised sections of society to be more productive. Towards this India requires innovations in education, healthcare, urban planning, public transport, waste management and rural housing? While we do not have to re-invent the wheel but new technologies should be developed to suit Indian conditions. In this context I am not talking of '*Juggad*' technologies alone but more substantive ones.

There are scores of examples of recent innovations by India in areas of space, computer software, automobile components, new drugs and health care facilities. For example, the performance of Indian Space Research Organisation (ISRO) is of global standards. The growing internet penetration in Indian cities and villages is another milestone of progress. India is a major power in information technology.

As a nation and as a civilisation, we have celebrated history of innovation commencing from Indus Valley Civilisation days. Our civilizational legacy of innovation in medicine and practices of yoga and naturopathy, logic and *sasthratha* (dialogue), philosophical quest and *sutras* are well known. Fortunately these attributes are of relevance in attaining excellence in the computer age.

Development and secularism must go hand in hand. Respect for another person's point of view as well as faith are an integral part of India's inheritance. It is this civilizational attribute, which I call Bahudha approach, that allows India to stand tall in the comity of nations and it is this which has facilitated India being home to all the major religions of the world. I would like to call the approach I am suggesting Bahudha. This comes from my personal attachment to an attitude that has greatly contributed to the enrichment of harmonious life in India: 'respect for another person's view of truth with hope and belief that he or she may be right.' This is best expressed in the Rigvedic hymn that enjoined more than three millennia ago.

Ekam Sad Vipra Bahudhā Vadanti

(The Real is one, the learned speak of it variously)[13]

Pluralism is the closest equivalent of Bahudhā in English. But Bahudha denotes much more than pluralism as *dharma* conveys more than religion. In short, the Bahudhā approach is both a celebration of diversity and an attitude of mind that respects another person's point of view. Democracy and dialogue are central to this approach.

In the wider context of values, "India that is Bharat" gives to her children: a simple living, strong family ties, and tolerance for other points of view, spiritual quest and respect for ecology. The Constitution of India sanctifies these values and provides a solid framework of 'rule of law' against 'rule by men.'

Innovations are taking place in the government, in the market and in civil society in media. The social and political process is getting increasingly interlinked, changing the character of the elites in the countryside.

The slogan "Sabka Sath Sabka Vikas" is most appropriate. It is and has to be inclusive and in conformity with our cherished values and principles of democracy and rule of law that the Constitution of

India enjoins upon the citizens and the government to adhere to. Tomorrow's India will be a country free of the scourges of poverty, hunger and illiteracy.

The health and robustness of a civilisation may be judged by its capacity to challenge and jettison the rituals and practices, opinions and beliefs which stifle progress and create divisions. The Indian civilisation has shown its resilience from time to time. It is my belief that as long as Indian society and polity encourage creative minds in the literatures and arts, science and technology, and give primacy to democratic institutions, to inclusivity and justice, India's age-old cultural strength would continue to be renewed.

AT THE END

I believe that both institutions and individuals are important. Institutions mould character and individuals provide resilience and flexibility to institutions. For to preserve and strengthen, hope calls upon our wisdom and our energy. The need is to nurture the moral strength of men and women and their leaders to live with compassion and to spend their energies working for inclusive development.

The Indian democratic system has always valued the integrity and conduct of its institutions as prescribed by the constitution and laws. In fact, during the last seven decades, India has not breached the constitutional banks except for a period of 21 months during 1975-1977 popularly termed as 'Dark Emergency Days.' the Indian Parliament continues to occasionally display intelligence in its debates reminiscent of earlier times. The rulings given by the Supreme Court of India are often cited by courts in the world by way of reference. The Indian press has produced some brilliant analysis on subjects of public interest. The members of the Indian Administrative Service, Indian Police Service, Indian Forest Service (all-India services) have performed their tasks well even in trying times. Our diplomats, the finance, revenue and audit officials command respect in India as well as outside India's borders. The civil society, thanks to information technology and social media, is taking more interest in public affairs than ever before.

We can draw some lessons from the manner in which 4 Asian countries acquired economic power: Japan, Singapore, South Korea and China. The Japanese miracle is largely due to their technological prowess and organisational abilities, Singapore through exemplary leadership and discipline, South Korea through new village development movement and strict enforcement of laws, and China on account of focussed government policy, leadership and the communist party. We in India have focussed leadership at the Centre and in several States. There is a high level of integrity at the Centre and several of Chief Ministers are persons of sterling integrity and committed to people's welfare and they belong to different political parties.

Let me quote a paragraph from my latest book titled *The 21st Century: Geo-politics, Democracy and Peace* (Routledge: New York-London **2017**). In this behalf:

"The real issue is: Is India moving forward? Are we indeed in a transition state moving towards better governance? I am inclined to answer in the positive. The political leadership, new awakening in the institutions of governance, independent character of judiciary, active media, and vibrant civil society and other institutions give me hope. This optimism is also based on the fact that the people of India, particularly the youth, want their institutions of governance to be imbued with sensitivity towards public aspirations and needs. Political executives, industry leaders, and government servants must pay heed. The non-negotiable and inescapable conclusion is that the government, civil society organizations, and the market need to act in concert. This is possible when we have harmony between forces of democracy, culture and administration."

I strongly feel that strengthening of open societies where dialogue has primacy and where the spirit of understanding another's point of view is cultivated leads to a better world. Fundamentalism or that a particular view of the world must prevail is the worst of all ideologies and must be discarded. The need is to resolve that as a people we will not allow our respective faiths to be used as instruments of violence. We must have the moral strength to live in accordance with the teachings of compassion and spend all our energies working for peace and development.

One is aware that a 'billion mutinies' are taking place almost on a daily basis in India. I am also aware that 'billion negotiations' are simultaneously taking place in the country of 1.3 billion people. The need is to exponentially expand the frequency and reach of these 'negotiations' to cover the entire population.

The world looks to India with respect for the manner in which we have permitted and practised a plural society. Our experience, in turn, should make us more concerned about our minorities and the weaker sections of our society. We must realize that only a democratic, secular India will command the trust of our own people, and also of the world.

IV

Fault Lines in Governance

– Yogendra Narain

When we were young I remember playing a game of "Touch me." We asked each other to touch us. If he touched our hand , we would say you have touched my hand but you have not touched me. If he touched my head , we would say you have touched my head but you have not touched me. And so the game went on because though my friend touched various parts of my body he could not touch ME, I consisted of all my body parts but also something more. Same is with governance. It is a nebulous concept which cannot be adequately defined. It consists of administration, policy making, judicial decisions, field implementation, decisions of officers under various laws, constitutional authorities, working of parliament, functioning of the political and administrative executive, working of financial institutions, law and order, punishment of criminals and so on. Governance is all this and yet something more. It can be experienced as bad or good, citizen centric or not, corrupt or honest , but it defies adequate definition.

The civil services and the political executive form an essential part of governance. The political leadership in a democracy provides the thrust for new policies and ideas. One of the reasons for the efficiency and effectiveness of the erstwhile Indian Civil Service (the ICS) was the generally high quality of leadership which it had to serve. The tasks which the leadership set for the Civil Services was clear and precise. This was because the leadership was highly educated, experienced, mature and knew the methods of achieving their goals. People like Vallabhai Patel were the product of a generation which understood the political environment and anticipated the problems which would be encountered in the implementation of the policies. His actions and leadership motivated the civil servants and brought about the integration of more than 561 princely states in the aftermath of Independence in 1947. With the enthusiastic support of the civil servants, Patel not only completed the integration of the States and steered the country through a critical phase but also re-erected the steel frame

However later the quality of political leadership declined. Extraneous considerations began to permeate the governance of the country. The requirements of principled and efficient governance were given a go bye. Political expediency and narrow personal interests dominated the national scene. Then a new terminology began to spread with dangerous consequences. This was the concept of the need for a "committed bureaucracy." A new division broke the unity of the civil services. While the concept of a committed bureaucracy could have been accepted if, the commitment was to serving the people with integrity and dedication, but it became anathema when it degenerated in to a commitment to political parties and particular political leaders. This added to the mistrust and hostility not only amongst the civil servants but also between the politician and the civil service machinery. The fallout of this development on the governance machinery was bound to be adverse. The political leaders were able to transfer the inconvenient civil servants and replace them with officers of their choice, with whom they developed an unhealthy nexus. This coterie then began to take patently corrupt decisions and were well protected.

These fault lines got further accentuated in the era of coalition governments. Whenever a situation arose where the ruling party did not have a majority of its own, the smaller parties on whose support the government existed, would demand officers of their choice. The ruling party is in no position to resist and governance became a casualty. Transfers of officials become so frequent that it becomes demoralizing.

The officers belonging to a particular caste look to Ministers of their own caste for advancement in their service career. They do not depend on their seniors to assess their work fairly and impartially and to look after their career prospects. The very rationale of hierarchical and disciplined bureaucratic structure has been undermined. In Uttar Pradesh, for instance, the Chief Secretary found that he was not even being called for the Cabinet meetings and his place had been suddenly taken by an officer, newly designated as Cabinet Secretary, a hot favourite of the then Chief Minister. This officer did not belong to any service but all files for the Cabinet had to be routed through him! This continuous demolition of existing and proven structures has led to unwanted fault lines appearing in governance

WORKING OF CONSTITUTIONAL AUTHORITIES

Our founding fathers, who wrote and adopted the Constitution of India, created in that basic document, several institutions, which constituted an essential part of it's basic features. These constitutional authorities and institutions were created by the Constitution, with the objective of ensuring democratic and responsible governance. Within the definition of Constitutional authorities come the President and Vice President of India, Parliament and the presiding officers, the Supreme Courts and the High Courts, the office of the Comptroller and the Auditor General, the Prime Minister and his Council of Ministers and similar structures in the States including the Governors.

These Constitutional authorities are different from the authorities created under specific laws or Government Resolutions like the Central Vigilance Commission, the CBI, the Human Rights Commissions, the Information Commissioners, the GST Council and such like institutions.

The Constitution has pinned great faith in the Constitutional authorities to oversee and sustain democratic governance in India. If these Constitutional institutions fail, then democracy is in danger. All constitutional authorities, except the President, are appointed by the President of India. The President is himself elected by the elected legislators both of the States as well as the Centre. His election symbolizes that the ultimate power in a democracy vests in the people and their representatives.

All constitutional institutions have to be manned by individuals. Therefore the effectiveness or ineffectiveness of these authorities depend on the choice of the people for that post. A wrong choice can make that institution lose it's credibility. Once credibility is lost the nation suffers as constitutional institutions and their working have wide ramifications. The ruling party in power must desist from committing the folly of selecting "its own men" for these constitutional posts. The selection should be of the best man available.

Recent events have thrown up the threats, both internal and external to the constitutional authorities The first and foremost being the functioning of the judiciary. The recent events, highlighted by the press conference by four senior members of the Supreme Court, in which the method of allocation of cases by the Chief Justice of India was highlighted, has put up a big question mark on the independence ,integrity and credibility of the apex court of the land. It has put a stamp on the unspoken rumours, both in the Supreme Court and the High Courts, that lawyers try to get their cases put up before benches of their choice, which can get them favourable decisions. This press conference further brought an undesirable differentiation between "important" cases and other cases. The issue of seniority of Judges in the Supreme Court also cropped up for the first time ever; the demand being that only senior judges should hear the so called "important" cases. If ever there was a case of contempt of court, this was the one.

Further more several lawyers tried to cow down the judges by shouting at them. All sorts of allegations and innuendos were hurled at the Chief Justice and his brother judges. That such action was being resorted to by senior lawyers was shocking. When the Chief Justice endeavoured to control the shouting, the lawyers trained their ire at him. The fault lines in the judicial system were showing. The senior lawyers were destroying the relationship between them and the judges.

Then the same set of lawyers attempted to further demoralise the Chief Justice by bringing a motion for his removal. When the motion was not admitted by the Chairman of the Rajya Sabha, the lawyers filed an appeal before the Supreme Court. When the Chief Justice set up a bench to hear the appeal, the lawyers said that the bench should not be constituted by the Chief Justice as the motion was against him! Who else was empowered to constitute the bench? This battle between the lawyers and the judges and the judges themselves caused a big dent in judicial governance in India.

Apart from this, the fact that more than 3.5 crore cases are pending in various courts at different levels has engendered a feeling in the citizens that perhaps the judiciary is not the best institution to sort out disputes. The courts are not showing a sense of responsibility by their conduct. Allegations of corruption are rampant from the lowest courts to the apex court. A former Law Minister went to the extent of submitting an affidavit naming the corrupt judges and yet no action was taken by the apex court.

The selection of judges by a "collegium" of senior judges in a most unscientific manner has raised questions of nepotism and favouritism. It was surprising that the Supreme Court decided to scrap the Judicial Accountability Bill, duly passed by the legislatures of all the States as well as Parliament. The setting up of the NJAC would in no manner whatsoever affected the independence of the judiciary. In USA judges are selected after appearing before the Senate, and getting it's approval, and yet the Court is considered independent. The Supreme Court, in setting aside the NJAC acted against the voice of the elected legislatures and has thus set itself on a path of confrontation with the Executive. The Executive has also held up appointment of Judges proposed by the collegium and thus a large number of vacancies are existing in all the courts of the country, thus further increasing the pendency of cases in the courts.

At the highest levels, for good governance, there has to be harmonious working both within the institution as well as between the institution and other constitutional authorities, We can ill afford any further fault lines between the constitutional authorities.

GOVERNANCE IN RURAL AREAS AND FARMERS

The present Government has announced their intention to double the income of farmers, efforts have been made in this direction such as crop insurance, loan waivers, efforts to raise the minimum support price to one and a half times the all inclusive cost of cultivation. But still the farmers are unhappy and have been giving expression to their unhappiness through protest, dumping of produce on roads, and suicides.

However fault lines that would emerge with this strategy is that if farm prices are raised without reference to global prices of agri-commodities, the result would be to push up food and industrial input prices way above global levels, creating a dragon the competitiveness of India's. economy as a whole

Agriculture strategies in the past were mainly focused on increasing agriculture production to improve self sufficiency and improve food security but did not explicitly focus on farm on farm income and farmers' welfare. Lack of irrigation facilities and low water use efficiency have led to low cropping intensity. It is expected that with emphasis on irrigation development under the Pradhan Mantri Krishi Sinchayee Yojana, the coverage of area under irrigation would be extended and "more crop per drop"will help in increasing cropping intensity. Higher cropping intensity will lead to higher farm income.

However at present the productivity of most of the crops in the country is below world average and much lower than agriculturally advanced countries. Between 1966-67 and 2016-17, though there was a 2.6 fold increase in the productivity of rice and a 3.5 fold increase in the productivity of wheat, the annual growth rate of foodgrains yield decreased from 3.2% in the 1980's to 1.9% in the 2010's

It is also necessary to rework the subsidy regime that hinders cultivation of crops best suited for particular agro-climatic conditions, such as by promoting sugarcane and rice in water stressed areas. It would be far better to give farmers income support rather than to subsidise particular inputs. Ending the stranglehold of the

Agriculture Produce Marketing Committees is also a must. The farmer should be free to sell wherever he wants.

Though almost sixty percent of the Central Budget goes for development schemes in the rural areas, the implementation of the schemes is left to various services like the Block Development Officers, the Panchayat Secretary, the Cooperative supervisor, the lekhpal/patwari and the Tehsildars the Junior Engineer attached to the Block etc. Nobody also knows how many schemes are being implemented at the village level. Some schemes are funded by the State Government, some by the Central Government, some by the local bodies, some by NGO's, some by Foreign agencies There is no single supervising agency to oversee these development schemes.

It is necessary to create an All India Rural Administrative Service for administering the rural areas. The existing IAS can look after the urban areas as well as Law and Order in the District. The All India Rural Administrative Service can be transferred from one State to another but should work in Rural areas only. This way specialization can be developed and the best practices of one State can be adopted by other States

NAXALISM AND MAOSIST MOVEMENTS

Naxalism has turned out to be a significant irritant to national development. With the persistence of the Maoist movement in Nepal, they have been able to develop a meandering corridor which is referred to as the Red Corridor. This corridor cuts through a swathe of Indian territory across the States of Bihar, Andhra Pradesh, Jharkand, Orissa, Chattisgarh and West Bengal. Though Naxalism started in West Bengal, it lost it's relevance there and has been now succeeded by the Maoist violence in the aforesaid States.

Official governance had ceased to exist in these areas though now the States have coordinated their strategies and slowly administration has reasserted it self. However Kangaroo Courts are still functioning in a clandestine manner, parallel to the paralysed State apparatus. 55 districts in the country are affected inspite of massive inflow of funds as well as armed personnel. Daily incidents take place leading to massive casualties on both sides. The root cause of this crisis is a corrupt political and administrative system. Popular unrest and youth anger is the result of a failed administration and the attendant administrative apathy.

Efforts have to be made to bring the Maoists and Naxalites back in the mainstream. The fact that the Maoists have achieved electoral successes in the recent past can be perceived as a cooption of the insurgents inside the political system and is thus a welcome sign. However the Naxalite affected areas near and about Dandakarneya, by and large, remain in the control of the insurgents, outside the contours of government departments, and this is clearly a fault line in an otherwise well knit administrative machinery.

DIVISIVENESS IN GOVERNANCE

Desmond Tutu had once said that "My humanity is bound up in yours, for we can only be human together." In a well administered state no individual can take the law into his own hands. However where policing is weak and characterized by slow response to complaints, people feel encouraged to turn vigilantes, especially when such vigilantism is perceived to have political backing. Lynching of cattle traders or alleged cattle thieves and such lynchings remaining unpunished pinpoint towards political connivance. Since the lynching is of persons belonging to a particular community a feeling of divisiveness has crept in society. It is very necessary to curb this feeling immediately otherwise it might lead to deeper cracks in the nation

KHAP PANCHAYATS AND FATWAS

In India, traditions and old customs firmly Rule. The Constitution is an attempt to create a modern society with the Rule of Law as the basic fulcrum. However in villages and closed societies people are not fully aware of the freedoms granted by the Constitution. They are not aware of the niceties of law. Feasting on this ignorance, the local influential persons take advantage and resort to arbitrary measures to retain their power and prestige.

The Khap Panchayats, which used to exist in the rural areas in the past, still hold sway and authority.

They decide on who can marry whom, whether inter caste marriages should be allowed, what punishment should be given to those who oppose their orders, whether Dal its can take out marriage processions and so on. Even the police show reluctance in initiating action against the members of the Khap Panchayats. The Supreme Court has clearly ruled that the orders of the Khap Panchayats are illegal but when the masses support such orders, the authorities are reluctant to have a showdown with them and the Rule of Law suffers.

Similarly the religious seminaries keep on issuing fat was on any issue that is brought before them. Such Fat was often go against all norms of a modern society but are followed by the masses. There was this case of a married woman being raped by her father in law. She was asked to first marry him, get divorced and then marry her husband. Here again the Rule of Law is replaced by rulings of religious bodies.

It is regretful that because of the need to garner votes, the governments in power are reluctant to strongly act against such bodies. They should, by law be banned.

ELECTION COMMISSIONS

We next come to the next most important Constitutional authority in a democracy. That is the Election Commission of India and the State Election Commissions. Under Article 324 of the Constitution, the superintendence, direction and control of the preparations of the electoral rolls for, and the conduct of, all elections to Parliament and to the State legislatures of every State and of elections to the offices of President and Vice Presidents is vested in the Election Commission of India Similarly for all Elections to the local bodies within a State, is vested in the State Election Commissions. The first general elections were held in 1952 after the preparations of the electoral rolls, throughout India. The Election Commission of India consists of the Chief Election Commissioner and two other Election Commissioners. The State Election Commissions have only one Election Commissioner.

These Election Commissioners are appointed by the Government. There is no laid out procedure for the selection of the Commissioners. No qualifications have been laid for the persons to be appointed. Unlike the judiciary there is no collegium which recommends the names either in the Government or in the Election Commission. There is no committee, which may include the Leader of the opposition or a member of the judiciary, which is involved in the selection. Since the appointments are made on the choice of the Government, in times of crisis, accusations fly thick and fast of the Election Commissioners favouring the Government. This happened recently when the dates for the Gujarat elections were announced by the Chief Election Commissioner, who happened to be a former Chief Secretary in the Government of Gujarat. Earlier accusations were made against an Election Commissioner, who was deemed to be very close to the Congress.

The toughest Election Commissioner we had was Seshan. He tolerated no nonsense from any political party and therefore was widely respected. However he came in conflict with the Government when the latter wanted to expand the then single member Commission into a three member Commission. A peculiar situation arose when Seshan went to court against the Government saying that the expanded Election Commission would be illegal, Two institutions of the Constitution were fighting with each other. Seshan had tasted power and he did not want to let go of it. This sullied the image of the Election Commission. Even after the Supreme Court endorsed the stand of the Government and two new Election Commissioners joined, Seshan never accepted them and this infighting was widely reported in the Press. The image of the Election Commission of India was severely dented.

Worse is the working of the State Election Commissions which were set up when the Constitution was amended in 1992 and the village Panchayats and Nagar Panchayats (Municipal Boards) were created under the amended Constitution. These State Election Commissions were given the mandate to conduct the Elections for the local bodies of that State. The State Election Commissioner is appointed by the State Government and is completely under it's thumb. The recent shameful case was that of the State Election Commission of West Bengal, where first the Commission extended the date of filing of nominations and then under Government pressure, withdrew the extension. The matter went upto the Supreme Court, which reprimanded the State Election Commission and asked it to invite nominations again.

Similarly in the case of the disqualification of Parliamentary Assistants to the Ministers in the Delhi Government, the Election Commission passed a hasty order, without hearing the opposite party, and recommended to the President cancellation of their appointment. This was rejected by the High Court of Delhi as the principal of natural justice was not followed, This badly affected the image of the Election Commission and allegations of towing the line of the ruling party were made.

Another Constitutional Authority which plays an important part in governance is that of the Governors in whom the executive power of the State is vested. They are appointed by the Hon'ble President on the advice of the Central Government. However the choice of the persons appointed is questionable. Though it was envisaged that they would be independent and unbiased in their dealings with political parties, it is not so. The action of Buta Singh, when he was Governor of Bihar, in recommending President's Rule, when Abdul Kalam was the President, drew ire of the Supreme Court, which ultimately rescinded the order. Similarly the action of Governor Bhandari in UP in the nineties, appointing the Chief Minister from a party, which did not command a majority, was adversely commented upon by the Supreme Court, which ordered fresh voting in the state legislature, closely monitored by the Court. Similar was the case in Jharkand, when the Governor appointed a Chief Minister, who did not command a majority. Recent actions of the governors in Goa, Karnataka and some North Eastern States, reveals a wide deficit in unbiased governance.

The conduct of politicians in power is also a disheartening feature of Indian democracy. The recent incidents involving the Chief

Minister of Delhi, who with some of his Cabinet colleagues, went on a dharna in the official residence of the Lt. Governor of Delhi, raises serious issues of protocol. Similarly in the elections in Karnataka and other States, the language used depicted the nadir of political vocabulary. Moreover the freebies announced at the times of elections has serious implications on governance. Free power for the agriculturists and the waiver of loans given to the farmers has economic implications for the entire nation.

As far as elections are concerned, at present they seem to be held almost throughout the year. Frequent elections hamper growth and development. Once the Model Code of Conduct comes into force, the government cannot initiate new policies as they would seem to influence voters. Even schemes that have been announced before the Model Code of Conduct came into force, but not implemented are to be put on hold till the election process is completed. The present Prime Minister has proposed that the country should adopt the policy of simultaneous elections. This will also reduce expenditure both of the Governments as well as the political parties. Government can then use these funds for development purposes

In 2011, the British Parliament enacted a legislation called the Fixed Term Parliament Act, 2011, by which elections have been fixed for every five years on a fixed date. This includes a device called a constructive vote of no confidence, by which a motion of no confidence would also mention as to who would be the next leader and Prime Minister. This measure will automatically ensure that elections are only held after a fixed term. USA already has this provision in its Constitution.

HEALTH AND EDUCATION

Health facilities in rural areas are negligible. The system of Primary Health Centres is not working because the Doctors after graduation want to work in urban areas where there are facilities of piped water supply, sanitation and electricity. Furthermore education facilities for their children if available, are of a low standard. Facilities in schools for girls, like girl toilets are few and far in between. The salaries of teachers, after the seventh Pay Commission, have risen sharply but the attendance of teachers is still very low. The teaching standards are deplorable and a recent study brought out that a student of class 8th could not solve the mathematics question of class 5. The Government has responded by setting up Sarvodyaya schools and Kendriya Vidyalays, but their presence in rural areas is limited.

Similar is the case of hospitals. The government hospitals are plagued by a shortage of funds, medicines and personnel. Private Hospitals have sprung up in huge numbers but are inaccessible to the poor because of the high costs. It is hoped that the new Ayushman scheme would fill the void to a large extent Our infant mortality rates and the maternal mortality rates, inspite of our best efforts, continue to be very high as compared to international standards. The fault lines, both in education and Healthcare governance, are clearly visible.

ECONOMY

Our economy has certainly grown by leaps and bounds. We are heading for a 3 trillion dollor economy, and have been rated as one of the fastest growing big economies of the world. However while the number of billionairs in India is tripling every year, the percentage of people below the poverty line continues to be high. Farmer suicides are still continuing. Farm production has gone up but farm productivity is low as compared to international standards. Migration from rural areas to urban areas is growing at a fast rate leading to stress on cities and towns. Enough jobs are not being created to absorb the University graduates,

Inspite of massive efforts by the Government, skill development to meet the demands of modern industries and commercial establishments is not keeping pace. This is leading to educated unemployment and represents a serious threat to the nation. One fault line in governance leads to another.

The political strategies we adopt today to meet such threats in India are like the methods we use to save our river protection works during the time of floods; one fault line is noticed and plugged. However, another fault line suddenly develops and our attention goes to plugging this new fault line and this goes on and on. Such a phenomenon is a persistent feature of developing countries and we need not get unduly worried about them as long as our governments are sincere and the people in the government continue to work, inspired by a spirit of nationalism.

V

India's Energy Security Challenges

– Sushil Tripathi and Lydia Powell

Introduction

According to the economic historian Angus Maddision,[1] China was the largest economy in the world in the 1500s followed closely by India with a Gross Domestic Product (GDP) of close to $100 billion each.[2] This economic order was maintained for the next three centuries with the great powers of the West well behind India and China in terms of GDP. In 1700, India had the strongest economy closely followed by China. India produced about 25 percent of world industrial output in 1750 but it fell to only 2 percent by 1900.[3] By 1980, India ranked ninth behind the United States and Western Europe in terms of industrial output but India was still 30 percent ahead of China which was ranked tenth. By early 2000s, India fell behind China whose share in global

[1]Maddison, Angus, 2008, The West and the Rest in the World Economy: Maddisonian and Malthusian Interpretations, World Economics, Volume 9, No 4, October-December.

[2]2015 US dollar in purchasing power parity; Cox, Wandell, 2015, 500 Years of GDP: A tale of two countries, New Geography, available at http://www. newgeography.com/content/005050-500-years-gdp-a-tale-two-countries.

[3]Clingingsmith, David & Jeffrey G Williamson, 2005, India's de-industrialisation in the 18 and 19 centuries, Harvard University available at https://www.tcd.ie/Economics/staff/orourkek/Istanbul/JGWGEHNIndianDeind.pdf.

economic output had grown to roughly 4 percent while India stagnated at about 1 percent.[4]

The causes of India's dramatic decline have been extensively researched and one of the widely accepted conclusion is that India lost out to competition especially from Britain which capitalized on the industrial revolution to undermine India's traditional advantage in textile manufacture.[5] Colonial repression not only prevented India from redeploying its resources productively in other sectors but also inhibited India's access to energy resources that was necessary for economic and military power. The socialist pattern of development that was adopted after independence did not help in reversing the course of decline.

But projections for 2050 and beyond show that the old economic order with China and India leading global GDP tables would be restored by 2040. According one report, China will account for 20 percent of the world economy by 2050 followed by India with 15 percent and the United States with 12 percent.[6] According to the OECD, India together with China is expected to account for about 42 percent of global GDP in 2060.[7] India is expected to be ranked second after China in 2060 accounting for just over 17 percent of World GDP. To realise the projected economic potential, India will have to grow rapidly in the next three decades which necessarily means accelerating energy consumption. The rest of the paper will explore energy fuels that are likely to power India's economic rise in the future and also analyse what this would mean for India's energy security.

[4]Srinivasan, T N. 2006. China, India and the World Economy, Economic and Political weekly, Volume 41, No 34 (26 August - 1 September).

[5]*Ibid*.

[6]PWC, 2017, The World in 2050: How will the global economic order change,? available at/https://www.pwc.com/gx/en/world-2050/assets/pwc-the-world-in-2050-full-report-feb-2017.pdf.

[7]OECD, 2014, GDP long-term Forecast, available at https://data.oecd.org/gdp/gdp-long-term-forecast.htm.

INDIA IN THE GLOBAL CONTEXT

Despite the impressive growth in India's energy demand in the last two decades, per capita energy consumption in India remains below world average energy demand. Estimated at about 630 kilogram oil equivalent (kgoe) India's per capita energy consumption is about a tenth of that in North America, a sixth of that in Western Europe and a fourth of that in China.[8] Low levels of energy consumption also imply low per capita GDPs and low rankings in human development indicators (HDI) (chart 1).[9]

To improve per person incomes and to advance human development, India's energy consumption must increase rapidly. In 2018, India's energy consumption is expected to grow by 4.2 per cent which is faster than all major economies of the world.[10] India is also expected to overtake China as the fastest growth market for energy by the late 2020s.

INDIA'S ENERGY SECURITY CHALLENGES

The close correlation between energy consumption, economic growth and human development means that the broad term 'energy security' has both a human security dimension and a national security dimension. In 1994, the United Nations Development Programme (UNDP) defined human security in terms of income security, food security, health security, environmental security, personal security, community security and political security.[11] Though energy was not mentioned in the UNDP report, the contribution of energy to human security can be explicitly linked to at least four of the six security dimensions (economic security, food security, health security, environmental security).

[8]World Bank, 2018, Open Database available at https://data.worldbank.org.

[9]Adhikari, Dipa and Yanying Chen, 2012, Energy Consumption and Economic Growth: A Panel Cointegration Analysis for Developing Countries, Review of Economics and Finance, 34, pp. 68-80.

[10]BP, BP Statistical Review of World Energy, British petroleum, 2018.

[11]UNDP, 1994, Human Development Report, New York: United Nations Development Programme.

Chart 1: Correlation Between Economic Development and Energy Consumption

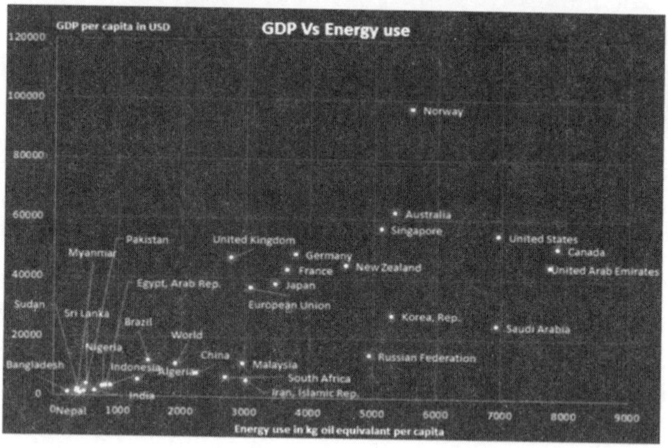

Source: World Bank database.

India's persistent effort to increase access to modern energy sources such as electricity and liquid petroleum gas (LPG) to poor households can be counted as major achievements in the human security dimension of energy security. Despite very low average household incomes, India is close to achieving complete electrification[12] of its households and also close to three fourths of its households adopting modern cooking fuels such as LPG.[13]

The national dimension of energy security which corresponds to India's ability to secure uninterrupted energy sources at an affordable prices remains a challenge. In the short term, the ability of India's energy system to react promptly to sudden changes in the global and domestic energy supply-demand balance remains compromised on account of entrenched government interventions in the sector.

Though many of the interventions are well intentioned and designed to address the problem of poverty in India, they have had an impact on long-term energy security that call for timely investments

[12]Kulshrestha, Ashish. 2018, India set to complete village electrification before target, Economic Times, 29 June 2018.

[13]Choudhary, Sanjeev, 2018, Nearly 80% of Indian households now have access to LPG gas, Economic Times, March 2018.

to supply energy in line with economic developments and environmental needs.[14]

INDIA'S ENERGY CONSUMPTION BASKET

India is the third largest energy consumer in the world accounting got about 5.5 percent of global primary energy consumption in 2016. Coal accounts for over 44 percent of primary energy supply estimated at about 890 million tonnes of oil equivalent (mtoe) and generates over 80 percent of all electricity supplied in India.[15] India accounted for 11 percent of the global coal consumption in 2016 and India remained the second largest coal consumer in the world after China.

Chart 2: Primary Energy Basket: India and the World (2016)

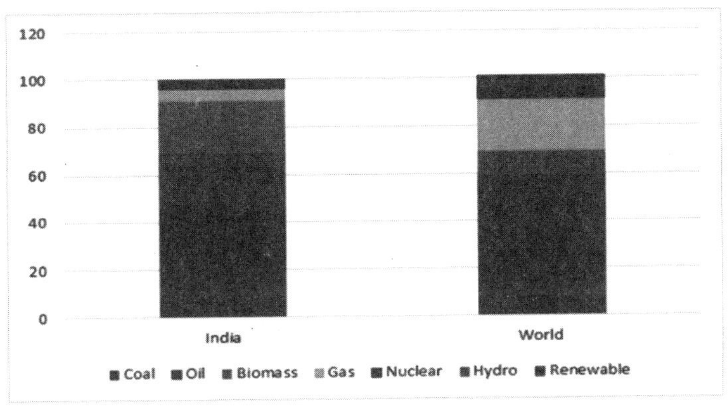

Source: World Energy Outlook 2017, IEA

Oil is the second largest source of primary energy in India accounting for 25 percent of primary energy supply. India is currently the third largest oil consumer in the world accounting for 4.6 percent of the global total. The third largest component of India's primary energy basket accounting for 22 per cent of the basket is surprisingly not natural gas but traditional biomass (firewood and other agricultural waste burnt as fuel for cooking). The fourth largest

[14]Definition of energy security by the International Energy Agency, available at https://www.iea.org/topics/energysecurity/.

[15]IEA, 2017, World Energy Outlook 2017, International Energy Agency, Paris.

component in India's energy basket is natural gas with a share of just over 5 percent of the total. The remaining 4 percent of the primary fuel basket is shared almost equally by nuclear power, hydro-power and renewable energy (chart 2).

As captured in chart 2, India's primary energy basket deviates from the world primary energy basket particularly in the share of coal with India having roughly twice the share of the world average and also in natural gas where the share is only about a fifth of world share. In a nut shell, this deviation characterises India's energy security challenges: single fuel dominance (low diversification with low share for gas) and a disproportionate share of biomass in meeting primary energy needs. The shape of India's energy basket is unlikely to change significantly by 2022 notwithstanding the ambitious target of 175 GW for renewable energy set by the current government.

However by 2047, the year that would mark the hundredth year as an independent country, India's fuel basket is likely to change significantly depending on India's policy choices and also on how technology evolves. Most projections for the business-as-usual scenario project the continued dominance of fossil fuels even by 2047 but ambitious scenarios that assume deep decarbonisation show a significant reduction in the share of coal on the assumption that the cost of new technology will decrease fast enough to enhance adoption rates.

KEY POLICY DIRECTIVES

The Integrated Energy Policy (IEP) prepared by the Planning Commission in 2006 addressed multifaceted energy problems the country must resolve to ensure efficient and sustainable use of energy, stating that 'India must pursue technologies that maximise energy efficiency, demand side management and conservation.'[16] For the first time, the IEP presented long-term goals for all energy sectors, not in an insulated and disconnected way, but rather in an

[16]Planning Commission, 2006, Government of India, Integrated Energy Policy: Report of the Expert Committee available at http://planningcom-mission.gov.in/reports/genrep/rep_intengy.pdf.

'integrated' and comprehensive manner. It also offered various scenarios based on different energy mixes and implementation of demand-side management. One of the key directions set for the long-term energy strategy was the validation of coal as a primary energy source for the long term and the necessity of ensuring coal supply with consistent quality. Power sector reform was strongly emphasised in relation to cost reduction and rationalisation of fuel prices. The approach for energy security was based on greater exploration or utilisation of domestic resources, namely oil, gas, coal, thorium and renewables. The IEP linked energy security with energy access, stating that 'India could not be energy secure if her people remain without secure supply for lifeline needs.' The IEP discussed issues of climate change and increasing environmental degradation in India, but made it clear that India would contain its carbon emissions if compensated for the additional costs involved.

Almost a decade after the IEP was proposed, the outcome is at best mixed. Even today India's energy sector is not fully capable of delivering secure supply of energy, even from domestic sources such as coal. In conjunction with a rising subsidy level and systemic failure to ensure proper revenue collection along the value chain, the financial capacity of energy sector players, especially in the power sector is significantly undermined. The outstanding debt of electricity distribution companies in India increased from about Rs. 2.4 trillion in 2011-12 to about Rs. 4.3 trillion in 2014-15.[17] Other sectors such as power generation also account for a high share of non-performing assets of the Indian banking sector. The Ujwal Discom Assurance Yojana (UDAY) scheme implemented by the government aims to improve operational efficiency and financial transformation of electricity distribution companies (discoms) but by many accounts the role of UDAY is likely to be limited to short term operational

[17]Patil, Mukta, 2017, Public opposition leaves loss-making electricity distribution firms powerless to raise tariffs, Scroll, 17 April 2017 available at https://scroll.in/article/834519/public-opposition-leaves-loss-making-electricity-distribution-firms-powerless-to-raise-tariffs.

improvement in discom finances. This means that deep rooted structural challenges will remain unaddressed.[18] Lack of sufficient capacity to make timely and adequate investments especially for natural gas infrastructure across the country has impeded the proposal to make India a gas based economy.[19]

On the other hand measures such as increasing sector wide energy efficiency, promotion of mass transportation, development of renewable energy have made substantial progress. More than 250 million LED bulbs have been distributed so far (with a target of replacing 770 million bulbs by 2019) with bulk procurement driving down costs and average household electricity bills being reduced by 15 percent where the bulbs have been installed.[20] Savings that will be achieved by sales of LEDs in India in 2016 are estimated to be comparable to the total electricity generated from solar PV in India in the same year. The Central Electricity Regulation Commission (CERC) has passed regulations to promote growth in the renewable sector, such as regulation on certificates for generation of renew-able energy and also regulation on renewable energy tariff-determination.[21]

Though the progress in developing nuclear energy has not met expectations since signing of the 123 agreement with the United States,[22] India has entered into arrangements with key suppliers of fuel and technology. Energy efficiency measures have also gained

[18]Chakravarty, P et al. 2017. Uday and Power Sector Debt: Assessing Efficiency Parameters and Impact on Public Finances, National Institute of Public Finance and Policy.

[19]PIB, 2016, Steps being taken to make India a Gas based economy, Press Information Bureau, Government of India, Ministry of Oil and Natural Gas, available at http://pib.nic.in/newsite/PrintRelease.aspx?relid=153957.

[20]IEA, 2017, World Energy Outlook 2017, International Energy Agency, Paris.

[21]Prateek, Saumy, 2017, CERC Releases Draft Renewable Energy Tariff Regulations for 2017-2020, Mercoindia, 17 February available at https://mercomindia.com/cerc-releases-draft-renewable-energy-tariff-regulations-2017-2020/.

[22]Ministry of External Affairs, 2008, Frequently Asked Questions on the 123 Agreement, available at https://mea.gov.in/Uploads/PublicationDocs/19149_Frequently_Asked_Questions_01-11-2008.pdf.

traction now that efficiency is part of India's national action plan on climate change.

The draft energy policy (NEP) released to the public in 2017 promotes the goals of energy access, affordability and sustainability which were also goals promoted by the IEP.[23] It proposes a co-ordinated strategy to achieve targets for electrification (universal "24x7" access for all by 2022), increase the share of manufacturing in GDP and reduce the share of oil imports. It also proposes creation of 175 gigawatts (GW) of renewable capacity by 2022, meeting the nationally determined commitments (NDC) to reduce the emissions intensity of the economy by 33-35 percent by 2030 (from the 2005 base line) and to boost the share of non-fossil fuel capacity in the power sector to 40 percent over the same period.

Projections by the draft NEP show an increase in the share of fossil fuels even by 2047 under the business as usual (BAU) and ambitious scenarios. However the draft NEP projects the share of fossil fuels in electricity generation to fall to about 61 per cent by 2040 under the BAU scenario and fall to just over 50 per cent under the 'ambitious' scenario on account of an increase in renewable energy. One of the key shortcoming that the draft NEP (2017) shares with the IEP (2006) is that both documents do not clearly prioritise or rank goals and policy options.

KEY PRIORITIES FOR ENERGY SECURITY COAL

The coal sector remains the most inefficient and least open to private investment, despite coal being the country's primary source of fuel. The near monopoly of public sector companies in mining and transport of coal obstruct the necessary increase of coal production and cause serious fuel shortages even when there is an abundance of domestic resources. Despite the reduction in growth of coal demand in the last two years, coal shortages continue to be reported. In the short term these are addressed through import of coal. India's coal imports stood at 217 million tonnes (mt) in 2017-18, higher than

[23]Government of India, 2017, Draft National Energy Policy, Niti Aayog.

212 mt imported in 2014-15.[24] This is despite the target set by the current government to eliminate thermal coal imports by 2018 and increase domestic coal to 1.2 billion tonnes by 2022.[25]

Chart 3: Coal Production, Consumption and Imports

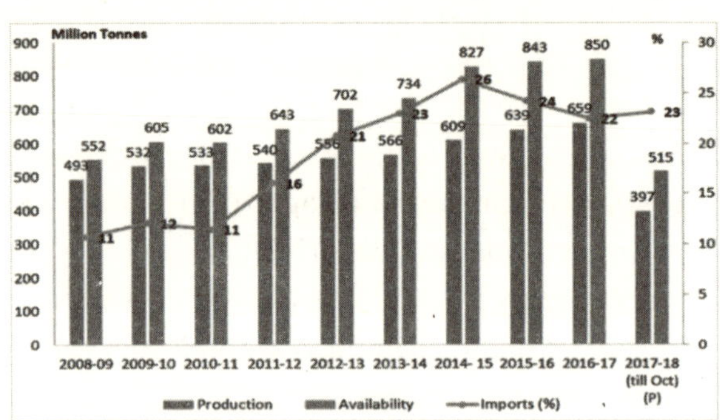

Source: Coal Controllers Office, Note: P- Provisional.

Reform of the coal industry must take into account the fact that certain rigidities that are locked up or institutionalised in the sector cannot be undone quickly. It may not be credible to expect that public sector monopolies would become more efficient through closer government intervention and target setting. In the absence of broad-based institutional reforms, demerging of the monopolies into several constituent companies and leaving them to thrive in an environment of friendly competition may be a viable option as suggested by the draft NEP.

Modernising India's coal sector is generally interpreted as an effort to increase the quantity of coal production through the participation of efficient and technology-savvy private players. Policies for captive mining in the mid-1990s and the effort to auction coal blocks in 2014-15 were driven by this goal. However, they have

[24]Mohammad, Noor, 2018, Four Years on, Piyush Goyal is Struggling to Wean India off Imported Coal, The Wire, 9 April 2018 available at https://thewire.in/energy/four-years-in-piyush-goyal-has-struggled-to-wean-india-off-imported-coal.

[25]PTI, 2017, Government plans to cut coal imports for power PSUs to zero, Press Trust of India 30 April 2017 available at https://timesofindia.indiatimes.com/business/india-business/government-plans-to-cut-coal-imports-for-power-psus-to-zero-in-fy18/articleshow/58442578.cms.

failed to live up to expectations. The history of auctions in India shows that self-destructive bidding is common, given that the cost of exiting or renegotiating a bid (or contract) is relatively low. Auctions for genuine commercial mining could bring the much-needed benefits of competition and efficiency in the sector. However, for commercial mining to be a success, mine operators will demand free-market pricing.

It is necessary to have a clear policy vision regarding the role for thermal generation in the short and medium term, and any required alteration in the role. This should be based on a periodic assessment of demand and supply options given current technology and price trends. If gas based generation is expected to meet peak demand and or act as balancing supply and coal-based capacity is likely to operate at lower plant load factors (PLFs) and perhaps also meet some of the variable demand, then these issues need to be studied further. Specifically, it is desirable that policy mechanisms should be devised to price capacity and availability, so that higher penetration of variable renewable capacity is possible without jeopardizing competitiveness of the industry or compromising on affordability.

Indian coal generally has low calorific value with high ash content, thus increasingly requiring washing with its attendant environmental consequences; it also implies that to deliver the same input heat value to thermal plants will require larger quantities of coal due to quality deterioration.

As economic and environmental benefits of coal beneficiation at the national level do not often translate into financial savings at the plant level, a case for justifying public support may be made. Such support will offer unambiguous support for shifting coal policy from quantity to quality.[26]

OIL AND GAS

Oil, in addition to being a constituent of India's total energy scenario, has a strategic importance for the country because of its irreplaceability for certain end uses, extremely high energy density, its

[26]Bam, S et al, 2017, Coal Beneficiation in India: Status and Way Forward, Special Report, Observer Research Foundation.

criticality in quick movement of heavy equipment and its use as a geopolitical tool. In the short to medium term, the demand for oil is likely to keep growing and its strategic position maintained.

India cannot fight geography and nature that have endowed only modest levels of domestic hydrocarbon (oil and gas) resources. While equity oil fulfils part of the need for a country's import concerns by neutralizing price (forex) volatility, it is only domestic production and storage that provides the complete strategic protection. The strategic importance of increasing domestic exploration and production needs to be clearly acknowledged in the policy as one of the touchstones in decision making.

At present levels of exploration India is viewed to have low prospectivity with very low exploration success ratio. It is therefore important that the country make extra effort not to leave any extractable subterranean hydrocarbon molecules behind. Towards this end, government decisions need to be based on commerciality of extraction indicated by the marginal value of the last drop extracted.

Chart 4: Oil Production, Consumption and Imports

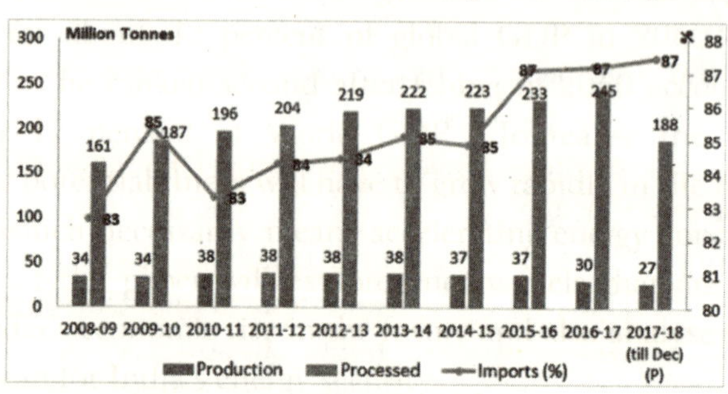

Source: Petroleum Planning and Analysis Cell.

The oil and gas industry should be viewed in totality of impact on national energy security rather than just another revenue generator for the government. Upstream is known to be risk intensive. A high risk venture requires high reward to cross the hurdle rate. In general, policy decisions need to be targeted towards lowering the costs of exploration. With challenging geology and generally smaller size of discoveries, it is obvious that exploration in India needs to be made attractive, else many areas are not likely to be bid and explored.

Hydrocarbon Exploration and Licensing Policy (HELP) has replaced the New Exploration and Licencing Policy (NELP) that has been applicable for the last 18 years. Under the new Open Acreage Licencing Programme (OALP), an investor interested in exploring hydrocarbons like oil and gas, coal bed methane (CBM) and gas hydrates may apply to the government to explore any new block (not already covered). The new policies will allow contractors to explore and produce all types of hydrocarbon (oil, gas, shale oil, shale gas, CBM, or any combination of them) under a single contract.

Exploration and production (E&P) has seen massive technology induction in the last decade and the trend is likely to continue. Using new technology is associated with additional costs and additional risks. As rightly observed in the draft NEP, India has generally been a consumer of new technologies rather than a producer for obvious reasons: low volumes, low number of participants, participant agility, risk taking capability of participants, ease of doing business and market freedom among other things. The Indian record in providing stable fiscal regime and access to product markets has not been sterling and this discourages new investors. At a policy level, certain stability provisions and safe guards need to be built in, so that complete economic life of the investment is enjoyed at stable terms.

As India has no choice but to import both oil and gas at international prices to meet domestic demand, it is only logical to offer the same international prices to domestic investors. A mechanism may be devised to limit the impact of volatility and high prices for crude oil. Just as OECD countries developed IEA to address challenge of OPEC, India and China as the growth drivers in oil imports should jointly work out a bargaining mechanism that tempers oil price volatility. Crude import dependence (Chart 3) is, to some extent moderated by export of refined products. In 2017-

18, net import of petroleum was reduced by 26 percent because of exports of refined products.[27]

Oil demand in India is expected to rise to more than 2 times comprising 24 percent of total energy mix in the next two decades.[28] The major source of increase in demand is expected from increase in transportation, increase use of LPG in households, higher income levels, increase in ratio of urban population, better road conditions that increase car ownership and planned industrial corridors.

In the context of imports, the biggest future constraint for India will be that of balance of payments problems arising from continuing growth of fossil fuels imports within which coal imports will may also occupy an increasing share. Crude oil prices are determined by global markets and as a large importer India has to adapt to volatility in prices. The shifting pattern of oil trade (from west to east) would necessarily mean changes in the how oil security is perceived by oil importing countries such as India how they expect to provide for it. By 2040, 70 percent of world's oil trade is expected to end in a port in Asia as the regions crude oil imports are expected to increase by 9 million barrels per day (mb/d).[29]

Energy imports accounted for over 32 of India's primary energy basket in 2015. The import of fossil fuels accounted for over 27 percent of total imports by value in 2016. Out of this oil accounted for nearly 67 percent.[30] India is currently the third largest importer of oil behind China and the United States, the fourth largest LNG importer after Japan, South Korea and China and the second largest importer of coal behind China. Roughly 80 percent of India's oil consumption, 50 percent of natural gas consumption and 15 percent of thermal coal consumption is imported.

[27]Data from Petroleum Planning and Analysis Cell, http://ppac.org.in/content/212_1_ImportExport.aspx.

[28]IEA, 2017, World Energy Outlook 2017, International Energy Agency, Paris.

[29]IEA, 2017, World Energy Outlook 2017, International Energy Agency, Paris

[30]ORF, 2018, Energy Database, Observer Research Foundation

Chart 5: Gas Production, Consumption and Imports

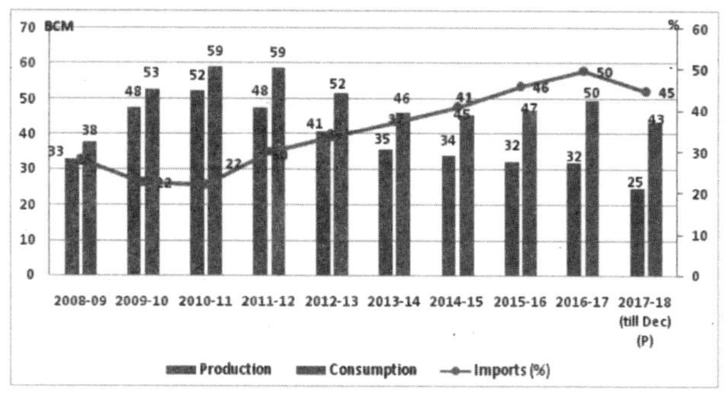

Source: Petroleum Planning and Analysis Cell.

The case of natural gas in India offers a telling example of the impact of policy on investment. During 2009-2016, India's primary energy consumption grew at a compound annual growth rate (CAGR) of 5 percent to reach 724 mtoe in 2016. However, the share of natural gas in the country's primary energy mix declined from 10 percent in 2009 to 6.2 percent in 2016 compared with the global average of 24 percent, mainly due to a sharp drop in domestic supplies. India's natural consumption of 39 cubic meters (m3) per person lags far behind the world average of 469 m3 per person.[31] Currently India is importing LNG to meet up to 45 percent of domestic demand. This trend of reduction in production in spite of reserves accretion and growing domestic demand clearly indicates that urgent steps need to be taken to make current gas production remunerative so as to incentivise investment in increasing production.

There has been a number of natural gas discoveries made neighbouring KG-D6 block in the east coast of India. Most of these fields are between 700 to 1700 meters deep which makes them technologically challenging and highly capital intensive. These would require specific incentives to attract investment. As per IEA estimations domestic production is expected to touch 90 billion cubic meters (bcm) by 2040 and majority of production is expected from ageing fields like Vasai. Indian demand for natural gas is expected to

[31]Conversation with gas industry players.

touch 170 bcm by 2040. Despite best efforts India is projected to have a gap around 80 bcm between supply and demand by 2040. This gap of demand will be supplemented by LNG imports. Since 2014 with the fall in gas prices in international market Indian LNG imports have increased by more than 30 percent.

The changes in the global gas markets characterised by abundant production and low prices can be leveraged if India liberalises its gas markets. An open and liberal market can facilitate the emergence of new gas trading hubs, and by the rise of so-called portfolio players–large companies with a diversified range of supply, shipping, storage and regasification options who can take different market positions with different risk profiles. The Indian government has proposed to develop a gas trading hub to effectively price domestically produced natural gas and incentivize the industry for further expansion of Indian domestic production of natural gas. India will need several LNG terminals and more commercially producible domestic discoveries to increase the domestic output and to develop a vibrant trading hub.

Gas could be one of the key sources of energy in Indian energy mix as it could act as a transition fuel which will help India in achieving its energy accessibility targets with low carbon intensity. The move towards a more diverse, flexible and liquid global gas market has important implications for investment and can bring significant benefits for India's energy security.

In energy systems heavily reliant on coal (as in India), where renewable alternatives are less readily available (notably in some industrial sectors and some states), and where seasonal flexibility is required to integrate high shares of variable renewables, gas based balancing capacity can play an important balancing role.

Gas-fired power plants could also make a difference in India for clean air in urban areas if the policy and regulatory environments provide the right incentives. The combustion of natural gas produces virtually no sulphur dioxide (SO2) emissions and negligible levels of fine particulate matter (PM 2.5), although it does result in significant levels of nitrogen oxides (NOX). In China, the near-tripling of natural gas consumption between 2016 and 2040 is expected to displace large quantities of coal, providing around 15 percent and 5 percent of the overall reduction in SO2 emissions and PM 2.5 (respectively) over this period. The impact is expected to be most pronounced at the local level, where gas is expected to provide part of the solution to the debilitating air pollution problems found in many large cities.[32]

Coal bed methane (CBM) resources are estimated to be 2.6 trillion cubic meters (tcm). These resources could be potentially much larger, as a few CBM block operators have experienced an increase in resource base following extensive field operations. India also has a favourable sub-surface setting in the form of multiple coal seams, which is not the case in other CBM – producing countries such as Australia and the US. CBM projects are promising but the low cost environment is inhibiting the growth of CBM capacity in India. India has a large shale potential but land availability and concerns of water contamination are the primary impediments for developing shale gas projects in India. Indian geology is thought to be not as favourable as US to commercially produce shale gas.

NUCLEAR ENERGY

Homi Bhabha, the father of India's three stage programme envisaged using uranium to fuel pressurised heavy water reactors (PHWRs) in the first stage followed by reprocessing spent fuel to extract plutonium. In the second stage plutonium was to be used in fast breeder reactors (FBRs) and the third phase involved the use of thorium in breeder reactors. The primary goal was to develop nuclear energy based on thorium of which India had abundant resources and replace uranium that was relatively scarce in India.

The Indian government is committed to its three stage programme despite many economic, technological and geo-political challenges. Due to earlier trade bans and lack of indigenous uranium, India has developed a unique nuclear fuel cycle to exploit its reserves of thorium as envisaged in its three stage programme. India's nuclear

[32]IEA, 2017, World Energy Outlook, International Energy Agency, Paris.

power program has thus proceeded largely without fuel or technological assistance from other countries. India's nuclear energy self-sufficiency extends from uranium exploration and mining through fuel fabrication, heavy water production, reactor design and construction, to reprocessing and waste management. It has a small fast breeder reactor and is building a much larger one.[33]

Out of a total capacity of 6780 MWe today, roughly a third are fuelled by indigenous uranium and the rest with imported uranium.[34] Following the Nuclear Suppliers Group agreement signed in 2008, the scope for sourcing both reactors and fuel from suppliers in other countries opened up. Civil nuclear cooperation agreements have been signed with the USA, Russia, France, UK, South Korea, Czech Republic and Canada, as well as Australia, Argentina, Kazakhstan, Mongolia and Namibia.

Between 2010 and 2020, further nuclear plant construction is expected to take total gross capacity to 21,180 MWe, though this time line is now extended and less than half that is likely by 2020. India's NDC to the Paris Agreement indicates that nuclear capacity would be increased ten fold to 63 GW by 2030. The draft NEP observers that nuclear energy is the only base load power source offering low carbon energy. India's import of uranium which accounted for only 0.2 percent of energy imports (in terms of value in US$) has substantially improved the plant load factor (PLF) of indigenously developed reactors. Today nuclear energy has the highest specific generation value (gigawatt hours of energy generated for megawatt of capacity) which makes it the most efficient mode of power generation in India. Renewable energy that accounts for over 60 GW or 18 percent of installed capacity contributes about 6 percent of power generation while nuclear power that accounts for less than 2 percent of capacity contributes over 3 percent of power generation.[35]

[33]WNA, 2018, Nuclear Power in India, World Nuclear Association available at http://www.world-nuclear.org/information-library/country-profiles/countries-g-n/india.aspx.

[34]*Ibid.*

[35]Calculated from Central Electricity Authority (CEA) database.

The efficiency of nuclear energy in providing clean uninterrupted power with a small land foot print highlights some of the advantages of nuclear power over renewable energy. Accelerating nuclear projects will not only meet India's energy security goals but also its environmental and emission goals.

HYDROPOWER

India is endowed with significant hydroelectric potential and ranks fifth in the world in terms of usable potential. As per the latest available data, India has around 44 GW of installed hydropower capacity.[36] This means that roughly 70 percent of the total capacity of about 148 GW is yet to be tapped. The share of hydro-power has come down from over 46 percent in generation capacity in 1966 to just over 13 percent today as a result of which adequate diversity in generation asset base between thermal and hydro power has not been maintained. This has affected India's least cost development strategy with over-reliance on 25-year old thermal plants and less reliance on 40-year hydro assets which generate power at less than ₹ 0.30/kWh.

Acquisition of land, environmental and forest clearance and resettlement of people affected by hydro projects have been major issues that have held up projects. There is also growing social and environmental opposition over damming and diverting the course of rivers. Transboundary rivers such as the Ganges, Brahmaputra and the Indus have issues of territorial sharing of water for irrigation and power. States with high hydro potential such as Arunachal Pradesh, Uttrakhand, Himachal Pradesh and Sikkim have tried to offer projects under a public-private partnership (PPP) model but they have not been able to progress primarily because of reasons listed earlier. In general, over 93 percent of the total potential in the north eastern region is yet to be tapped, primarily in parts of the Brahmaputra river basin. The scenario is in sharp contrast to the southern and the western regions where more than 65 percent of the potential has already been harnessed. Addressing social and

[36]Calculated from Central Electricity Authority (CEA) database.

environmental issues with the care they deserve may allow some projects to progress.

RENEWABLE ENERGY

For the first time since the climate talks started in 1992, there has been a market shift that indicates the potential to decarbonise the energy sector in India.

Chart 6: Power Generation Capacity 2017-18

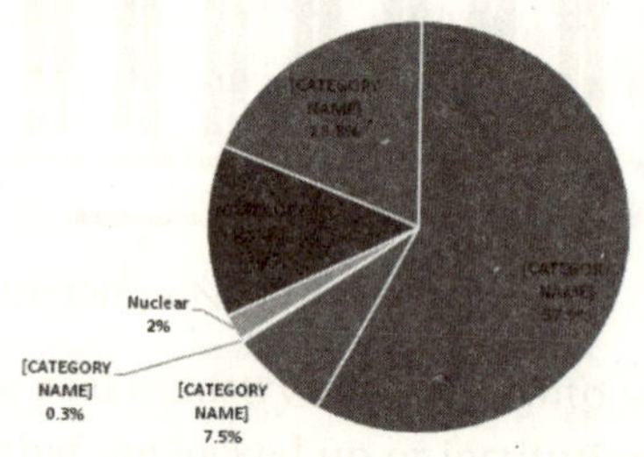

Source: Central Electricity Authority.

The current market trends show that the renewable energy costs have come down significantly in the last 10 years; solar photovoltaic (PV) costs have reduced by 20 percent annually since 2007. Some projections on future costs indicate that solar PV will be the cheapest source of electricity in India by 2020 and solar rooftop system with battery back-up will achieve grid-parity by 2025.

The policy environment in the country is also conducive to the renewable energy (RE) sector. A preferential tariff and subsidy programme for renewables, concessions given by several states for reduced transmission and distribution charges are among several policy initiatives that have contributed to the considerable growth of the sector in the country. In addition, Renewable Purchase Obligations (RPOs) require electricity distribution companies to purchase a percentage of power from renewable sources. Tariffs have been one of the most important factors in pushing renewable energy forward.

It is also estimated that between 2016-17 and 2031-32, for every 1 MW of coal power plant installation, 4.5 MW of solar and wind capacity will be installed. With solar power tariffs for larger projects hitting as low as Rs 3/kWh (US₵5/kWh), decreased wind power tariffs, and improved storage technology, it is likely that investors prefer to invest in renewable energy as it guarantees long term policy support with assured long term returns.

Chart 7: Power Generation By Fuel (2017-18)

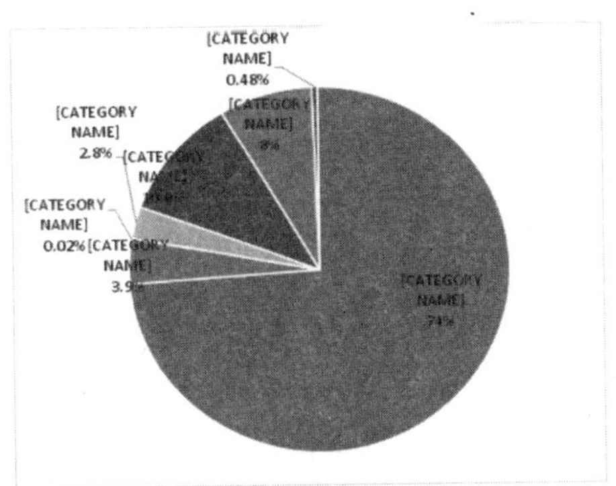

Source: Central Electricity Authority

Electricity is the primary vector for RE but the electricity sector in India faces serious financial challenges. The fundamental difficulty with RE integration is the stochastic nature of electrical flows. Distribution companies (discoms) do not merely form the last mile of supply of electricity but they are the only cash flow generating part of the electricity value chain. Given the incessant variability of power load and the vagaries of commodity prices, the need for discoms to adapt is now greater than ever. This is compounded by the fact that there exists no easy way of transmitting cost of electricity to end users in a dynamically changing environment. Having a robust distribution system has become even more challenging in the face of influx of renewables and the possibility of having multiple distribution entities within the same geographical area.

The government and other actors who are participating in the electricity value chain need to acquire new assets such as state-of-the-art weather prediction and forecasting systems from which data can be fed directly to grid operators from Power System Operation Corporation Limited (POSOCO) to regional Load Dispatch Centres (RLDCs and SLDCs). Furthermore, the ability to couple this prediction data with varying demand patterns and interpreting the results with sophisticated analytical engines will become necessary to guide grid operations. The national balancing area for RE integration as proposed by the draft NEP may be too large. National scale balancing may not only bring up state-centre issues but also require huge investment in technology.

To ensure that human errors are minimized, fail-safe automated decision making and control systems will have to be put in place to cater to rapidly changing grid conditions. To provide for back-up of RE systems it is necessary to create spinning reserves of coal and gas, grid operators will have to be able to bring these reserves online or off line based on grid stability requirements in five minute intervals. System operators will need to update their grid operation protocols grid codes to ensure that stochastic flows generated due to RE systems do not affect grid adversely. Some mechanism of a centralised forecasting, pooling and coordination will have to be devised so as to ensure seamless wheeling of power between surplus and deficit regions. These are not merely technological challenges but also financial challenges.

In order to level the playing field between conventional and renewable power, the current practise of socialising the cost of intermittency and variability of RE should be phased out. The draft NEP reflects this view and proposes the withdrawal of 'must-run' status and other support such as capital subsidies, non-levy of interstate transmission charges etc for renewables. The assumption is that when consumers become agnostic to the source of power, markets rather than policy would decide which power would be despatched. While support mechanisms such as 'must-run' etc are distortions the biggest source of distortion is the fact that RE tariff is not based on two part tariff that is applied to conventional power. This requires a detailed discussion on the creation of capacity markets and energy markets, a complex issue that even Germany is yet to resolve. The suggestion to move beyond RPOs and (Renewable Energy Certificates) RECs is a step in the right direction. System level cost of RE rather than 'levelized' cost of energy (LCOE) must be taken into account while evaluating competitiveness of alternative sources of power.

CONCLUSIONS

While India's energy and economic growth accelerates, India's ideal path could reflect that of Japan, a net energy importer like India, which has achieved high levels of economic and social progress without proportional increase in energy consumption on account of the emphasis on efficiency of energy use. Japan's energy intensity (energy use per unit of GDP [PPP]) decreased by 24 percent since 2000 which is 17 percent lower than the average for G 7 countries.[37] In contrast India could also follow a high energy intensity path if the emphasis on domestic manufacture succeeds. This may result in higher incomes and better living standards but it would come at the cost of higher domestic and global pollution levels. Net energy exporters such as Saudi Arabia have shown high energy consumption as well as high energy intensity but without proportional increase in economic output. Between 2000 and 2011 energy consumption in Saudi Arabia grew faster than GDP leading to an increase in total energy intensity which was against the worldwide trend of decreasing energy intensity.[38] Development based on energy intensive industries such as refining and petrochemicals along with energy intensive lifestyles (partly on account of climatic conditions in the region) are cited as reasons for high energy intensity in Saudi Arabia. For India, that seeks to follow a path based on manufacturing, (Make in India)[39]

[37]Motherway, Brian, 2017, The Global Evolution of Energy Policy and its Implication for Japan, International Energy Agency, Paris.

[38]Dubey, Krarti M.K. and Howarth N. 2017, Evaluation of building energy efficiency investment options for the Kingdom of Saudi Arabia, Energy, Vol: 134 pp: 595-610.

[39]Government of India, 2018, 'Make in India' policy details available at http://www.makeinindia.com/home.

this could mean a high energy consumption and high energy intensity path. However energy options open to India to follow a high energy and high energy intensity path are tempered by the perennial trade deficit which limits India's energy imports and also by the global mandate to limit the emission of carbon. A path that balances these concerns is likely to be more secure than the one that does not.

Historically India's energy concerns have been dominated by external supply risks–particularly oil supply risks–because these were closely linked to two of India's key strategic interests-national security and rapid development through economic growth. India's response consisted of traditional policy interventions such as self–sufficiency, stockpiling and development of non-fossil alternatives such as nuclear power and renewable energy. Today qualitative concerns that include equitable access and environmental integrity are demanding equal, if not greater emphasis than quantitative concerns in India's energy security strategy. Finding the right balance between often competing demand for quantity and quality will decide India's energy security.

VI

National Security and Internal Security

– Mahendra Kumawat

"Internal Security is the foundation for peace and development of the nation."

Since Independence, India has faced several grave internal security threats including communal holocausts, secessionist movements, militancy, violent farmer and student agitations, caste-conflicts, pro–and anti-reservation movements, and left-wing extremist movement. Over 33,000 policemen have martyred to protect integrity of the nation and to maintain public order. Incidentally, the term 'internal security,' which is an element of 'national security' has not been defined in any official document of the Government of India. As it happens, neither has the term 'national security.' Conventionally, national security implied physical or geographic protection and was thus largely equated with 'national defence.' However, the definition of national security has expanded over time from territorial defence to protection and preservation of the core values and vital interests critical to the nation state from external and internal challenges and threats.

Internal security, a sub-set of national security is therefore concerned with threats and challenges emanating from within a country having potential to adversely affect public order and security of the nation. Currently, India faces an array of grave internal security threats: insurgency in Kashmir and Northeast, Naxalism, Terrorism including cross-border terrorism, illegal migration, communalism, organized crime etc. Then there are emerging internal security threats such as cyber crime, environment including water related conflicts, unemployment and internal migration related conflicts, and mob violence in the form of lynching.

AN OVERVIEW OF INTERNAL SECURITY CHALLENGES

Kashmir: A Simmering Cauldron

No state of India has suffered from internal turmoil as well as attacks from across the frontier than the state of Jammu and Kashmir. Before India's independence, the state remained free from communal violence and other large-scale conflict. However, taking advantage of widespread organised conflict in Poonch, a tribal invasion, aided and abated by Pakistan, was launched in the first-half of October, 1947, which escalated into the first Indo-Pak war (1947-48). Yet again, Pakistan waged full-fledged war in 1965 and a battle in 1999 to wrest Kashmir from India. However, it failed in its mission every time.

The militancy in 1990s was the worst period in the history of Kashmir when terrorists from across the frontier–supported by the Pakistani army–indiscriminately targeted not only security forces but also the opinion makers, ideologues, social activists, politically affiliated people and religious minorities ,which resulted in deaths of over 40000 people including over 13000 civilians and 4000 Security Force personnel. Security operations contained militants' violence significantly around 2006 when PM Manmohan Singh government initiated a number of measures for restoring normalcy and economic development of the state. Confidence Building Measures (CBMs) included commencing of bus-service in Srinagar-Muzaffarabad and Poonch-Rawalkot route; and Cross Line of Control trade between J&K and Pakistan Occupied Kashmir. However, the period of comparative peace was short lived.

Violence again gripped the valley in the wake of the Amarnath land issue in 2008 and large scale protests and police firings in 2010 which led to death of over 120 people-mostly youth. The killing of Burhan Wani, a young militant and a poster boy in July 2016 revived militancy in a big way.

There are new worrying trends namely people's demand for 'Azadi,' local youth joining militancy in larger numbers, a sea of mourners in the funeral processions of militants, people obstructing security forces operations, stone pelting by youth including girls students, etc. It is widely believed that militancy in the Valley has evolved into insurgency which poses a formidable challenge to the state.

After the imposition of Governor's rule in July, 2018, the security forces have increased counter–insurgency operations. Will this strategy help? Argues security expert David Kilcullan,

"At the start of a conventional engagement if we are facing one hundred of the enemy and we kill twenty, we can assume that eighty are left. In counter-insurgency, this logic does not hold: the 20 killed may have 40 relatives who are new in blood feud with and are obligated to take revenge on the security forces who killed the 20, so the new number is 120."

So what then is the resolution to the Kashmir conundrum? One argument is to increase security forces stationed in Kashmir, which is already one of the most militarised areas in the world. Security forces may well bring down violence but will not resolve the tangled problem in which all the three stakeholders- Indian state, people of Kashmir and Pakistan are sticking to their stated or unstated policies.

In such a scenario, besides continuing security operations, the state need to work for winning hearts and minds of the people of Kashmir by granting greater autonomy, repeal of AFSPA from the areas where the army is not deployed, development at greater pace and good governance. Talks with Pakistan to convert LoC into international border and to borrow a phrase used by former PM, Manmohan Singh, 'making borders irrelevant' (by increasing movement of people and trade across the LoC) may bring back peace and normalcy in this strife torn paradise on earth.

Insurgency in the North Eastern States

The North Eastern region comprising of eight states is of great strategic importance. Except Sikkim, all other states have witnessed intense insurgencies and violence at one point of time or other. In fact, the situation n North Eastern States especially in Nagaland, Mizoram, Assam and Manipur had been grave and threatened integrity of India. Presently, Mizoram, Tripura and Sikkim are free from insurgency but the remaining states namely Assam, Arunachal Pradesh, Manipur, Meghalaya and Nagaland are still affected by criminal activities of insurgent groups albeit much less than at any time in the past. This became possible due to security operations against insurgent groups coupled with the policy of negotiations with them resulting in Suspension of Operations (SoO), Memorandum of Settlements (MoS) and Ceasefire agreements.

Notwithstanding significant improvement in the security situation, acts of kidnappings, extortions, killings of security personnel and of the cadres of rival groups continue to beset with the region. More important, the demand for Greater Nagaland—a very sensitive and complex issue is yet to be resolved. It is not clear how the present regime intends to settle it. Whether the solution will be acceptable to Nagaland, Manipur and Arunachal Pradesh is to be seen.

What is needed is to deal with the armed cadres of different banned groups engaged in criminal activities like extortions, kidnappings and killings, etc., effectively and explore political solutions to the vexed problems of the region. Rapid development coupled with emotional integration of the people of the Northeast with the mainland India will be a lasting solution.

Left-Wing Extremism

India has a long history of extremism emerging from the far left ideologies. Soon after launching of the Communist Party of India (CPI) in 1925, an armed struggle was put into practice in the Telangana Region (then a part of Hyderabad Kingdom) in 1946. After the merger of Hyderabad into India in 1948, more than 50000 armed personnel were deployed by the Government of India to deal with the movement. It is estimated that 4000 communists and peasant militants were killed. The movement continued till October 1951.

The second left extremist movement in India known as the Naxalite movement originated in Naxalbari area of West Bengal in 1967 and it continues. In its over half-a-century long existence, the movement has shown tremendous grit and resilience. At its peak in the last decade after the merger of Peoples' War Group (PWG) and Maoist Communist Centre (MCC) in 2004 (the united outfit called the Communist Party of India, Maoist) its influence spanned 223 districts across 20 states, although of course, the degree of activity varied vastly. The CPI (Maoist) carried out big attacks on police armouries, jails, police camps and caused heavy loss of life and property. Jehanabad (Bihar) Jail break (November 2005), attack on Nayagarh Police armoury, police station (February 2008) and Sukma, Chhattisgarh (April 2010 in which 76 CRPF men were killed) are among the worst attacks.

Owing to a slew of concerted measures taken by the Central and State governments especially after the creation of Naxal Management Division in the Ministry of Home Affairs (MHA) like raising of a new force Commando Battalion for Resolute Action (COBRA) on the pattern of Greyhound–an acclaimed commando force of Andhra Pradesh, besides providing over 120 Battalions of Central Armed Police Forces (CAPFs) to the Naxal affected states, financial assistance to states to raise India Reserve Battalions and development in the Naxal affected states, there is a significant improvement in the situation.

Though the Naxalite movement once described by Manmohan Singh, former Prime Minister as 'the worst internal security threat that India ever faced' has been considerably contained the fact remains that it is still a menace in 35 districts of 7 states namely Chhattisgarh, Jharkhand, Odisha, Maharashtra, Bihar, Andhra Pradesh and Telangana.

What is prognosis of the Naxal Movement? So long as severe disparities in level of living, heavy incidence of unemployment, lack of economic opportunities, continued exploitation of disadvantageous segments of society and atrocities on the weaker sections, persist, the Naxalite problem is not likely to totally eradicated. The problem, therefore, will have to be tackled by adopting a multi-pronged integrated strategy. While coordinated and stringent security operations are necessary, simultaneous imaginative and radical administrative, political and developmental measures are imperative to remove the Socio-economic malaise which has sustained the movement.

Terrorism

The scourge of terrorism has impacted nations across the world and India has been among the worst hit. Ministry of Home Affairs has banned 39 terrorist organisations. Some of the worst terror strikes which shocked the world are: Mumbai (March 1993, 257 deaths, 717 injured), Coimbatore (1998, 58 deaths, 200 injured), Attack on Parliament (2001, 9 killed), Akshardham, Gandhinagar (2002, 30 deaths), Delhi (Oct 2005, 62 deaths), Varanasi (2006, 21 deaths), Mumbai (2006, 209 deaths), Malegaon (2006, 40 deaths), Panipat (Samjhauta Express, 66 killed), Hyderabad (Aug 25, 2007, 42 killed), Ahmedabad (July 2008, 29 deaths, 110 injured), Delhi (Sept 13, 2008, 33 deaths, 110 injured), Guwahati (Oct 2008, 81 deaths, 470 injured).

But the terror attack on Mumbai on 26thNovember, 2008 by sea-borne terrorists of Lashkar-e-Taiba from Pakistan, which claimed 163 lives and injured 239 shocked the world like never before as the victims were from across the world-USA, UK, Japan, Israel, Canada, etc.

The 26/11 Mumbai attack forced Central and State Governments to revamp intelligence agencies and creation of 'National Investigation Agency.' Private business establishments like shopping Malls, hotels, etc. also improved their security. All these measures have yielded good results. But cross-border terrorism sponsored by Pakistan Army and ISI continue to bleed India in Kashmir and elsewhere. Islamic State is also striving to make its presence in India. The need, therefore, is to establish 'National Counter Terrorism Centre' (NCTC) to prevent terror attacks as the mandate of the NIA is only to investigate terror attacks once they have taken place.

Communalism

If one single cause that has played havoc in the life our nation, it is the bane of communalism. The communal seeds sown and nurtured by the British caused vivisection of Indian Subcontinent. The partition unleashed a human tragedy hitherto unseen, in the world history. It is estimated that two million people were killed and 15 million people migrated in both directions under great hardship. Father of the nation was also assassinated by a communal bigot.

Sadly, the virus of communalism did not die down in free India. Quite a large number of communal riots have rocked different parts of India in past seven decades, the worst being–Moradabad (1980, 1500 deaths), Nellie, Assam (1983, 1819 deaths), Delhi (1984, 2733 deaths), Bhagalpur (1989, 1161 deaths), Gujarat (2002, 1267 deaths). Incidences of communal violence continue to bleed India as a following chart would show:

Number of persons killed and injured in communal violence

Year	Number of persons killed	Number of persons injured
2014	95	1921
2015	97	2264
2016	86	2321
2017 (up to May)	44	892

Source: Reply to the Lok Sabha on 8 August, 2017.

Not surprisingly, India was ranked 4th in the world in 2015-after Syria, Nigeria and Iraq–for the highest social hostilities involving religion (Huffington Post, 14 April 2017)

Being acutely aware of India's widening communal fault line, President Obama during his visit to India in 2015 cautioned, 'India will succeed so long as it is not splintered along the lines of religious faith ... and is unified as one nation.'

Communal harmony in India has been mainly vitiated by political leaders to garner votes. Fundamentalists have also contributed to this malaise by their impassioned rhetoric.

Communalisation of Police

The police, being a part of the society that it operates in, has also been affected by the virus of communalism. Even in the aftermath of partition when communal violence was at its peak, many policemen affected with this malaise did not try to avert riots; rather they too participated in it. A number of commissions which were appointed to enquire into the communal riots have lamented about this creeping threat. Khushwant Singh in his book, 'The End of India' quotes observations of Justice Madon who enquired into the riots in Bhiwandi and Jalgaon in 1970 about the nefarious role of politicians and policemen in perpetrating as well as dealing with the communal violence:

"It was a lonely, arduous and weary journey through a land of hatred and violence, of prejudice and perjury. The encounters on the way were with men without compassion, lusting for the blood of their fellow men, with politicians who trafficked in communal hatred and religious fanaticism, with local leaders who sought power by sowing disunity and bitterness, with police officers and policemen who were unworthy of their uniform, with investigating officers without honour and without scruples, with men committed to falsehood and wedded to fraud and with dealers in mayhem and murder."

Many years later, the Srikrishna Commission which inquired into riots in Mumbai in December 1992-93 had also, inter-alia, brought out the factors which had contributed to the lack of effectiveness of police. These included, among many others, Communalisation of Police. Madhav Godbole in his well researched work 'The Holocaust of Indian Partition–An inquest' quotes the relevant part of the report of Srikrishna Commission:

"The evidence before the Commission suggests that in some measure at least there has been polarisation in the police force on communal lines.... It is true that the policemen is a constituent of society and cannot avoid being impressed (sic) by the communal influences in the society in which he lives. While communal thinking in an ordinary citizen, however objectionable, may not produce immediately visible pernicious results, communalisation of a policeman has that effect."

To overcome the malaise of communalisation in police, Madhav Godbole writes, the Central Government constituted on 7th Oct 1992 a new wing of the Central Reserve Police called Rapid Action Force (RAF) to render assistance to the states.

Organised Crime as a Threat to Internal Security

The menace of organised crime has emerged as a grave internal security threat. Way back in 1993, N.N. Vohra Committee made startling revelation that 'the network of Mafia is virtually running a parallel government.' Elaborating on the nexus between mafias, bureaucrats, politicians and judiciary, it mentions:

"The big smuggling syndicates, having international linkages have spread into and infected the various economic and financial activities including Hawala transactions, circulation of Black Money and operations of a vicious parallel economy causing serious damage to the economic fibre of the country. These syndicates have acquired substantial financial and muscle power and social respectability and have successfully corrupted the government machinery at all levels and wield enough influence to make the talk of investigating and prosecution agencies extremely difficult; even the members of judicial system have not escaped the embrace of the Mafia."

In the past quarter century, the multi-headed monster has gripped almost every aspect of national life. For instance, now there are mineral mafia, sand mafia, water mafia, examination mafia, etc.

Strangely, only two states (Maharashtra and Delhi) have specific law to combat the organised crime. The National Investigating Agency (NIA) created in 2008 has not been mandated to investigate organised crime. Nor is there any national agency collecting information about a variety of criminal syndicates operating in more than one state and to advising states for co-ordinated preventive action.

The most sinister development in the recent times is that mafia who hitherto provided only financial and muscle support to politicians are now themselves joining politics and many of them have entered into state legislative assemblies and Parliament.

Illegal Migration

Speaking in the Parliament former Dy. Prime Minister, L. K. Advani described illegal migration from Bangladesh as the most dangerous and creeping internal security threat. It is estimated that India has around 20 million illegal migrants from Bangladesh who have settled in different parts of India.

However, the impact of illegal migration has been most marked in Assam and Tripura. While it has changed electoral balance in many districts of Assam, the majority of tribal population of Tripura at the time of independence has been turned into a minority. Lt. General Sinha, then Governor of Assam, described illegal migration from Bangladesh as 'demographic invasion' of Assam. No wonder on this issue Assam faced a bloody insurgency (1979-1985) which seriously threatened integrity of India. The question of four million people excluded from the National Register of Citizens in Assam recently has potential to turn into yet another internal security challenge.

Realizing gravity of the threat posed by illegal migrations from Bangladesh, the Government of India has taken series of measures which inter alia include: a dedicated border guarding force–BSF, to guard 4096 km. of Indo-Bangladesh border, creation of over 2000 km long distance fence along the border, construction of border road and Border Area Development Program (BADP), etc.

However, despite these measures illegal migrations has not fully abated on account of the porous border (more than a thousand kilometres border being riverine and due to other reasons is, still unfenced)

It is, therefore, imperative that the border guarding mechanism be further strengthened by speeding up the construction/erection of the fence, resettlement of the people residing about 100 villages right on the border at least five hundred meters inside Indian territory and stop diversion of the BSF for other internal security duties, etc.

Water-Brawls to Water-Wars

"Water may become a more significant source of contention than energy or minerals out to 2030 at both the intra-state and inter-state level."

Global Trends 2030: Alternative Worlds
A publication of the National Intelligence Council, USA, 2013

Water has been the *raison d'être* for the rise and fall of human civilization. It is said that the next world war will be fought on water issues. India has water disputes with its most neighbours—Pakistan, China, Nepal and Bangladesh. Within India, the inter-state river water disputes are among the most contentious and emotive issues. Karnataka and Tamilnadu have often been rocked by violent agitation over the Cauvery water dispute.

Daily brawls over water are common occurrence/sights in slums of cities and towns all over the country. Road blockades and protests for supply of water are also common in summer months. A few years ago, police had to resort to firing on farmers agitating for water resulting in death of four farmers in Sriganganagar district (2004) and five farmers in Tonk district (2015).

In this backdrop, NITI Aayog reports that "India is facing its worst water crisis in history and that demand for potable water will outstrip supply by 2030" portends ominous situation. In such a scenario, water crisis is emerging as one of the foremost internal security threats is a distinct possibility. Therefore, Central and State governments must take all possible measures to save India from plunging into water related civil- wars.

Youth Unemployment and Internal Migration: An Emerging Internal Security Challenge

India has almost added 1000 million people to its population since independence in 1947. Today, it has the largest number of youth (356 million in the age group of 10-24 as per a 2014 UN report). What does it signify? In this regard, a research finding of Harvard Kennedy School is instructive:

"When 15-24 years olds made up more than 35 per cent of the population as is common in developing countries, the risk of conflict was 150% higher than with a rich country age profile."

Sadly, a majority of our youth lack employable skills. This vast reservoir of youth is always available for agitations–be they are for reservation issue or for the ban of a film like Padmavati.

A large number of unemployed youth migrate north to south since the socio-economic development of the southern states is considerably higher and that attracts people. As per the 2011 Census, 46.4 million people migrated from economically less developed states to more developed ones between 2001-2011, and mostly to southern states. Internal migrations have been cause of conflict in 1960s. Assam witnessed a violent agitation against 'Marwaris.' In Maharashtra, Shiv Sena spearheaded a movement against people coming to Mumbai in search of jobs from other states. In 29 August, 2007 Hindi speaking workers were killed in Karbi Anglong district of Assam and recently Shillong, Capital of Meghalaya, witnessed a violent agitations against the Sikhs who migrated there a long ago.

Therefore, the unskilled youth bulge-mostly unemployable has many facets impinging on internal security which call for imaginative solutions at the national level.

Cyber Security

Advent of Computers and internet have profoundly affected every aspect of life. In fact, it is all pervading. The 21st Century is rightly called the cyber-century. The technological revolution has fundamentally altered the way we live, work and relate to one another. In the scale, scope and complexity the transformation is unprecedented in human history.

Indians are among the top users of smart phones and internet. The number of smart phone users is estimated to hit 317 million by the end of 2018.

While it has positively affected every walk of life, there are attendant threats looming large on the horizon initially in the form of cyber crime and finally cyber war. Articulating about dangers posed to cyber security, PM, Narendra Modi says, "Clouds of a bloodless war are hovering over the world."

As far the impact of IT on internal security challenges is concerned, it has added to the complexity of every issue be that organized crime, terrorism, insurgency, communalism, public agitation, etc. For instance in Kashmir the present upsurge in insurgency owes a great deal to use of social media like WhatsApp and Facebook by militants and the local people. In no time everyone in the valley learns about security operations and killings of militants which bring instant protests and stone pelting on security forces Burhan Wani's joining militancy and his killing in 2016 gave a great impetus to insurgency, mainly due to the use of cyber media. No wonder there are frequent stoppage/curtailment of internet services in the valley to maintain public order. In Rajasthan, recently internet services were stopped for two days to ensure smooth conduct of an examination.

Organized criminal syndicates especially drug mafia have opened 'Internet-Pharmacies' to sell drugs on line. ATM and credit card frauds are rising. Hate videos are going viral.

Cyber Crime is a new phenomenon and preparedness of the states' police forces is uneven. While Southern states and metro cities have taken some measures, most police stations in India lack expertise to tackle this growing challenge. The Central and State governments must invest in human resources and infrastructure to improve investigative skills of policemen across the country.

A ROADMAP FOR ROBUST INTERNAL SECURITY SYSTEM

In the past seven decades, the Indian Police has faced a number of grave internal security challenges. Measures were taken by the Central and State Governments to improve functioning of internal security system comprising of the Central and State Police forces, infrastructure and laws to tackle the ever increasing internal security challenges. Specialised forces have been raised to combat specific challenge: Border Security Force (BSF), Central Industrial Security Force (CISF), National Security Guard (NSG), Indo-Tibetan Border Police (ITBP), Rapid Action Force (RAF), Commando Battalions for Resolute Action

(COBRA), National Investigation Agency (NIA), Greyhounds-An anti-naxal force of Andhra Pradesh, etc. Enactment of specific laws like National Security Act, Unlawful Activities (Prevention) Act, The National Investigation Agency Act, Information Technology Act, etc. are some of the measures in this direction.

In the aftermath of 26/11 Mumbai Attack, Coastal security received greater impetus. Not with standing the above measures taken by the MHA and the State Governments from time to time, fact remains that these were piecemeal and after crises and not as a part of Internal Security doctrine and concomitant strategy. The following suggestions will go a long way in improving internal security system as well as in making Indian police SMART.

SMART is an acronym coined by Prime Minister Modi for police which means Strict and Sensitive, Modern and Mobile, Alert and Accountable, Reliable and Responsive, Techno savvy and Trained.

Re-organisation of Ministry of Home Affairs (MHA)

India is perhaps the only country in the world where the key sovereign function-maintenance of internal security which requires undivided attention, is one of the many functions of a ministry (Ministry of Home Affairs) since it is burdened with a large number of subjects unconnected with internal security. There is no justification to have matters such as official language, warrants of precedence, appointment of Governors, Creation of new states, inter-state boundary disputes, pension to erstwhile rulers, rehabilitation of people affected by disasters, natural calamities and man-made disasters, Padma Awards, etc. in the charter of MHA.

It is imperative to have an exclusive ministry—Ministry of Interior, to deal with a range of complex and burning and burning issues relating to internal security. Further, there is need for specialists to be given senior positions in the ministry at the level of joint secretaries and above.

Police Reforms—A Mirage

Successive surveys on police reveal peoples' general dissatisfaction and complaints against the Indian Police of unprofessionalism, high-handedness, corruption, burking of crime, custodial torture, etc. This is not surprising since the police that the British created was 'to rule' rather than 'to serve' the people evidently, there are many areas which call for urgent reforms. Unfortunately, very little has been done in this regard. Prakash Singh, a former Director General of Police, BSF and a crusader for Police Reforms expressed his anguish thus:

"There have been any number of commissions, both at the state and central levels-State Police Commissions, National Police Commissions, Gore Committee, Ribeiro Committee, Padmanabhaiah Committee, Malimath Committee, to name only a few- which made recommendations for reforms, but these received no more than cosmetic treatment at the hands of the government with the result that there has been hardly any change in the colonial policing which we inherited from the British."

On quite a few occasions, the Supreme Court of India has expressed dismay and dissatisfaction over the indifference to the issue of police reforms. In fact, the directions of the Supreme Court have consistently been stonewalled. It is, therefore, imperative in the national interest that the Government of India passes a Central Legislation on the lines of the Model Police Act drafted by Soli Sorabjee committee incorporating therein the directions of the Supreme Court. The State Government should also comply with the directions of the Supreme Court and establish 'State Security Commissions,' 'the Police Establishment Board' and 'the Police Complaints Authority' among others which will go a long way in making Indian Police-people friendly, accountable and a professional service.

The Number Crunch

Indian Police, both Central and States is 3.61 million strong. However, the police-population ratio (192 policemen per one hundred thousand of population as on 1 January, 2017) is one of the lowest in the world. UN recommended 230 policemen per 100,000 people. Coupled with this, the vacancy position is enormous (21.8% as on 01.01.2017). Therefore, the actual strength available for general policing (maintenance of law and order crime investigation) and internal security duties is grossly inadequate.

Indian Police

	State Police Forces	Central Police Forces	Total
Sanctioned Strength	2.464 million	1.154 million	3.618 million
Actual Strength	1.926 million	0.987 million	2.913 million
Vacancy	0.538 million	0.167 million	0.705 million

Source: Bureau of Police Research and Development.

Despite huge vacancies, the recruitment process is highly irregular. Thus in 2016, only 71,711 policemen were recruited as against the total vacancies exceeding 0.7 million! States generally fill up vacancies in an election year with an eye on votes rather than the actual requirement.

Irregular and large scale recruitment in one go affects quality of personnel recruited, training, promotions and therefore morale, and more importantly the policing itself including maintenance of internal security. It is, therefore, imperative that the Governments both Central and States conduct police recruitment annually taking into account the vacancies that would arise after three years as the process of recruitment and training takes at least three years. Incidentally, the importance of annual and planned police recruitment was stressed upon the Chief Ministers by former PM, Manmohan Singh in the Internal Security Conference in 2007, but only to be ignored by most of the states.

Training

Though training is of great significance for imparting necessary skills and knowledge, it is the most neglected aspect especially in the State police forces. A quality Audit carried out by BPR and D-2016 revealed a number of serious deficiencies namely, inadequate number of trainees, lack of motivation and suitable qualification of trainers, inadequate infrastructure, etc. Irregular and large scale recruitment in a particular year adds to the existing problems of the training institutes which in turn affects quality of the basic training. Ill trained policemen cannot be expected to cope with the challenges they are required to face.

In the fast changing world it is imparting that the policeman are given in-service training from time to time. However, at the cutting edge level i.e. constables who constitute over ninety percent of the force, in-service training is imparted after 15-20 years and there too emphasis is on physical training. The need of the hour in Democratic Republic is to lay greater emphasis on the constitutional ethos, human rights and scientific aids to investigation, both during the basic as well as in service training of policemen.

Modernisation of Police Forces

Modernisation of police forces including police stations is crucial for meeting the current and emerging internal security challenges. The scheme for Modernisation of Police Forces (MPF) initiated by the MHA in the year 2000 is a significant initiative towards capacity building and improving infrastructure. However, the allocation of amount has been reduced considerably (chart below) over the years.

Funds Allocation under Police Modernisation by MHA

S. No.	Financial Year	Annual released funds (in billion Rs.)
1.	2013-14	13.38
2.	2014-15	13.97
3.	2015-16	6.61
4.	2016-17	5.92
5.	2017-18	1.32

Source: MHA Annual Report 2013-18.

The State police forces are always short on funds for improving infrastructure, mobility and training. The reduction of funds by MHA is likely to affect their modernisation programmes. The Union Government, therefore, must enhance the amount under this scheme.

Need to Strengthen Co-ordination Mechanism

The 26/11 Mumbai attack clearly brought out lack of co-ordination between different agencies of the Central and State Governments. Neither the Intelligence input given by the Intelligence Bureau to the Maharashtra Governments was acted upon nor did Intelligence Bureau follow it up with the state after conveying the intelligence input. Coast Guard authorities who had earlier detained and later released sea borne terrorists, did not inform the State police or Central Intelligence agencies about it. The result: ten terrorists could wreck havoc and cause mayhem in the financial capital of India.

It is for the political and bureaucratic leadership of the nation to ensure effective coordination between different agencies and SFs concerned with the national security.

Need for Modern Laws and Internal Security Doctrine

It is an irony that India which aspires to be a super power, its criminal justice system of which the police is a part, and the first responder to tackle internal security challenges, continues to function within the legal framework provided by the British in the nineteenth Century. No wonder that it takes decades for courts to decide even simple cases. People therefore lose faith in the criminal justice system and take law into their hand. Lynching and mob-violence are visible symptoms of the fast eroding faith of the people in the rule of law.

The Indian Police Act 1861 has remained unchanged despite demand from police professionals and directions from the Apex Court. There is no central law to deal with Organised Crime which is a serious internal security challenge. The Private Detective Agencies (Regulation) Bill is pending in the Parliament for the last eleven years. Drones are likely to be misused by the terrorists and anti-social elements but there is no law on horizon to deal with the challenge.

Lack of a national security doctrine including internal security doctrine allows political leadership to buckle under pressure and take decisions which erodes rule of law. Withdrawal of criminal cases against the supporters of the party in power by State governments has become a new normal.

Summing Up

How robust is our internal security system? Have we taken adequate measures to revamp police and security forces? Are we addressing the root causes of internal security challenges? The answers may not be flattering. There are several weaknesses in India's internal security setup, as described in this essay.

There has also been a disproportionate allocation of finance to deal with security challenges. Mandarins in the North and South Block at Raisina Hill may recall that China's internal security expenditure ($123.65 billion) exceeded its defence budget ($119 billion) in 2012.

Further, India has lacked comprehensive security reviews of its preparedness and responses to internal security threats. A case in point is the 26/11 attacks in Mumbai. While the United States appointed a commission to look into what went wrong during the 9/11 attacks, there has been no such body appointed by the Government of India. Where there have been other commissions and committees to inquire into various communal riots, violent public agitations and police reforms, not enough cognizance has been given to the recommendations made by them.India needs comprehensive internal security reforms instead of the usual piecemeal reactionary measures in the wake of every crisis.

BIBLIOGRAPHY

Annual Report 2017-18, Ministry of Home Affairs, Government of India.

Crime in India 2016, National Crime Record Bureau, MHA.

Data on Police Organizations (As on January 2017), BPRandD, MHA.

The 9/11 Commission Report, WE Norton and Company, New York.

India Vision 20-20, National Planning Commission, Govt. of India, 2004.

Public Order, Fifth Report, Second Administrative Reforms Commission, Govt. of India, 2007.

Khushwant Singh, The End of India, Penguin.

Ayaz Memon, Ronzone Banerji, India 50, The Making of Nation, Book Quest Publishers, Bombay, 1997.

Madhav Godbole, The Holocaust of Indian Partition: An Inquest, Rupa and Co, 2006.

Global Trends, 2030: Alternative World, National Intelligence Council, USA Publication, 2012.

Initiatives for Peace and Development in Jammu and Kashmir, MHA, Government of India, 2006.

Neil Padukone, Security in a Complex Era: Emerging Challenges Facing India, Observer Research Foundation Publication, 2016.

Balraj Puri, Kashmir: Insurgency and After, Orient Longman, 2008.

David Kilcullen, Counter-Insurgency, Oxford University Press.

VII

The Environment Vision and Challenges

– Ajay Shankar

The reality of the state of the environment in India is truly disturbing. India has14 of the 15 cities in the world with the highest levels of air pollution. It is fourth from the bottom in the ranking for environment performance. As much as 78% of the sewage generated in cities is untreated and flows into rivers and lakes. Of the household waste being generated only about 82% is collected and of this only about 23% is treated. The problem of plastic waste strewn across the country is increasing and has become critical. Chemicals, especially pesticides, are getting into the soils and into the food chain. The avoidable health costs are rising for all as a result of environmental degradation.

A positive transformation of the environment has been seen in many countries over the past few decades. In each case it has been driven by a national consensus at a critical juncture to do what it takes to fix a major environmental challenge, such as river pollution, or, air quality and also to incur the additional costs required. Then implementation mechanisms with sufficient empowerment followed.

In London in the winter of 1952, as many as 12,000 people died in the Great Smog. It led to concerted measures including the enactment of the Clean Air Act and subsidies for phasing out the use of coal for household heating in London. Today, it is difficult to imagine the smog over London and that it caused so many deaths. The river Rhine, which flows through many countries, was known as the 'open sewer of Europe' in the seventies. A Rhine Action Plan was adopted at the Ministerial Rhine Conference in 1987. This was the result of demand for action for cleaning the river gaining momentum and support from key stakeholders reaching a critical threshold. Most of the goals which were to be achieved by 2000 were actually reached before 1995. The Rhine was transformed into 'the cleanest river of Europe.' More recently, Mexico and China have shown substantial improvements in air quality within the space of a few years.

Fortunately, national capacity in India for major achievements and transformations have been increasing by leaps and bounds over the decades. The success in space is universally recognised. A more recent example is the success in solar energy. India launched its National Solar Mission in 2010 and adopted the target of having 20,000 MW (Mega Watts) of solar power by 2022. This had then appeared highly ambitious as solar power installed in the country was just about 160 MW. The price of solar power was over four times the cost of power from conventional sources of energy. The fiscal resources for subsidies for such a large programme were just not available. But India, to the surprise of many, began to succeed exponentially and by 2014 it had already installed over 2,500 MW of solar power. It now has an installed capacity of 23,000 MW, having achieved its original 2022 target four years ahead of schedule. The target has since been made far more ambitious and the aim is to get solar capacity to reach 100,000 MW by 2022. Though highly challenging, this appears attainable. This again shows that if India decides to have real ambition, it can surprise itself and the world.

It is time for India to have national purpose and ambition for succeeding in setting the environment within the country for its own people right. India now has the late mover's advantage.' The key environment management technologies have been getting better. The real costs of these have also been coming down. The best can be accessed easily in this globalised world economy. India should, therefore, be able to do what it takes to clean up the environment in a few years. Technological and management capacities within India have also been improving and are becoming world class. But it would need a clear articulation and strong political commitment both at the

Center and in the States to give transforming the environment in its totality the highest priority. Through a transparent consultative process clear goals and feasible measures for achieving these goals would emerge. This would lead to a realistic assessment of the financial and management resources as well as regulatory changes that would be required. Agreeing on ambitious target dates for achieving specific outcomes would be the key step.

The following could be considered as ideal goals for India at 75 in 2022.

Air quality would be brought down to permissible limits across the country.

All sewage would be treated.

All household solid waste would be collected and treated in accordance with prescribed standards.

Water quality of all rivers and water bodies would be restored.

Soil contamination would cease.

Once there is a national consensus with full political commitment for achieving these highly ambitious goals, progress in meeting the challenges of creating the requisite implementation mechanisms, provision of resources, capacities of program and project implementation, effective monitoring and evaluation systems would follow. In the government system clear targets do drive outcomes as is being seen in the recent large national programs for toilet construction, Ujjwala for provision of cooking gas cylinders and Soubhagya for getting electricity to all households.

Of all the environmental goals the most immediate and urgent task is to address the challenge of air quality. The air quality of Delhi is the worst among major cities of the world with the particulate matter (PM) in the city being on average 4 times above the safe limit. Air pollution is the fifth largest killer in India. The country has the highest death rate in the world from chronic respiratory diseases and asthma. It has been estimated that poor air quality in Delhi damages, irreversibly, the lungs of 50% of all its children. This is actually a health crisis which needs a National Mission to address it.

While the knee jerk reaction of odd even tried out by the Delhi government did not really help, a holistic approach which takes into account all available technological options and associated costs would be the right way to proceed. The objective should be to bring PM levels down within permissible levels and, that too, at costs which are affordable in five years. China has recently demonstrated improvement in air quality by 30% in some of its most polluted cities in the last few years.

The most important transformations as far as air pollution is concerned are already under way. The ongoing investments to upgrade the quality of petrol and diesel to conform to BS VI standards are nearing completion. Supply of BS VI quality fuel by 2020 would be a reality. These are at par with present day European standards. In theory, pollution from vehicles on our roads should then come down to European levels. However, for this to actually happen something would need to be done at the same time about those older vehicles which even with BS VI fuel they would still continue to pollute the air in an unacceptable manner. If nothing is done about the older polluting vehicles, then in a normal business as usual scenario it would take about ten years for a substantial impact on air pollution to be seen. Through the normal process of slow attrition, the old vehicles would get replaced by newer vehicles and it would take many years for a sufficiently large number of old highly polluting vehicles to stop being used altogether. Getting vehicles above a certain age off the roads in Delhi is on the anvil. However this would have not much of an impact. Delhi is at the center of a much larger National Capital Region. Air pollution does not recognise city boundaries. Vehicles move across cities and regions. Hence the problem of all old polluting vehicles across the country would need to be addressed now. What is likely to work best would be a judicious combination of the carrot and the stick. A substantial fiscal incentive for trading in a vehicle above a prescribed age for a new one would work well. The exemption of all taxes on the new vehicle being purchased when an old one is returned would be an attractive enough incentive. The government would actually forego revenue only on the additional sales that would take place as a result. There would be no budgetary outgo and, therefore, this decision should not be so difficult to take. Foregoing notional revenue is far easier than providing actual budgetary resources. Dealers would be required to take the old vehicles in exchange. The automobile companies should be required to set up a network of yards where these old vehicles would be scrapped in a modern environmentally sound manner conforming to good global practices. Traceability of actual scrapping of each vehicle would need to be put in place to ensure that the system is not misused. Initially only all old trucks, buses, tempos and three wheelers above a certain age should be targeted as these contribute the most to air pollution. At the same it should be announced that after the window of three years scrapping of these vehicles would be mandatory along with some punitive measures for non compliance.

The World Health Organisation (WHO) has drawn attention to the health hazard posed by the use of diesel. There is no similar caution about petrol. The discussion on phasing out of diesel has started in the West. While these are early days, it would be good if Indian experts joined the ongoing international conversation on the issue of diesel. If the science about the adverse health effects of diesel is unambiguous then phasing out of the production and sale of diesel vehicles would become necessary. India should not be a latecomer on this issue.

Electric vehicles do not pollute the air on the road at all. The world is moving swiftly towards large scale usage of electric vehicles. London and many other cities are considering mandating that from a future date, all new vehicles would have to be electric. Our own EESL (Energy Efficiency Services Limited of the Ministry of Power) has done commendable pioneering work with the first round of bulk procurement of electric cars. Two Indian companies, Tata and Mahindra, are the suppliers. (All global car companies are gearing up for the electric car. Volvo has announced that they make only electric cars in the future.) These cars are being leased for use by government on the same commercial terms as are in use for normal cars hired for official use. The good news is that EESL is being able to run these cars without any subsidy as they were able to get attractive enough prices for the cars through bulk procurement. This means that a benchmark price for the electric car for viable non subsidised running as a taxi has already been set. Real prices should only go down with larger volumes. To address air pollution, Delhi and other highly polluted cities could take the decision that from next year itself all new permits, including replacement permits, for public transport; buses, taxis, and three wheelers would be given to electric vehicles only. They should set up a sufficiently large network of public charging stations in advance so that there are no long queues as is still the case with LNG stations. For the taxi operator actual costs would need to be kept down to the same level as for normal vehicles for them to make the switch gladly. This could be achieved for taxis, three wheelers and mini buses by fixing a reasonable enough rate of supply of electricity to the charging stations and regulating their margins. Only electric buses are still very expensive in comparison to normal buses. These would need to be given a subsidy to make their running viable. Such a subsidy program for electric buses for city running would be well worth it. There is a useful precedent also. At the time of the global financial crisis in 2008 the central government gave a large number of city buses at its own cost as a pure demand stimulus measure. This would make a dramatic impact within three to five years on air quality in the cities. The maximum impact would be in those smaller towns where polluting tempos are the sole means of public transport. As these get replaced by electric mini buses, air quality should start getting down towards permissible levels rapidly.

There is one other factor which has a major impact on the air quality especially in Northern India and that is the burning of crop residue from cultivation of paddy in rural areas. Appealing to farmers not to do so has not and is not going to work. Nor would a ban on burning. Such a ban is unenforceable. Efforts are being made to persuade the farmers to plough the waste into the soil to enhance soil nutrients and productivity. If this succeeds on the scale needed, the problem gets resolved. But getting farmers to change habits is not easy. They may still see the costs of doing so outweighing the benefits. However, an out of the box approach of using the market mechanism should work. If a remunerative enough price for the crop residue is offered, the farmer would find it worth his while to incur the cost of pulling out the waste and selling it. NTPC took a commendable initiative by inviting bids for supply of briquettes made from crop residue with the intention of adding this to coal in their thermal power stations and using it to generate electricity. This approach could be extended as an immediate measure to buy all the crop residues presently being burnt as briquettes and using it in the thermal power stations along with coal. This would take care of the problem fully. Even if briquettes made out of crop residue are a bit more expensive, the impact on the tariff would at best be a few paise. This increase would be permitted by the regulators. The thermal power stations should therefore not find it too much of a burden to do this.

Alternative possible uses of crop residues through decentralised gasification for generating electricity, or, getting methyl alcohol as a fuel for transport could conceivably become environmentally and commercially better options in the future after R&D and demonstration pilot projects. In case this happens, these can then be promoted. The cost would be the ultimate determining factor and the price mechanism would need to be used by the state to get the transitions to take place.

All households are in the process of getting access to clean cooking energy through electrification under Saubhagya and provision of cooking gas cylinders under Ujjwala. This is a huge transition which is transforming the quality of life of all rural households and especially of women. The provision of life line energy consumption for cooking at rates which the poor can afford through subsidies, or, cross subsidies would help in completing the full transition to the use of only clean energy for cooking. Otherwise, the poor may have the gas cylinder and the electricity but not be able to afford using these for cooking and continue to use cow dung cakes and fire wood. Subsidised supply at affordable rates is amply justified on account of the health benefits to women from using cleaning cooking energy and what it would do to the quality of life of the household with the elimination of indoor air pollution. India would also achieve a major SDG goal. Subsidy would also be justified on account of reduction in overall air pollution in the country. Burning of biomass for cooking is a major source of air pollution.

With the transition to clean cooking energy taking place, cow dung would becomes available as an energy resource for decentralised generation of electricity at the village level. It's use could be promoted by the Electricity Distribution Companies by deciding to buy this electricity at an attractive enough price asa feed in tariff. This would drive private investment and generate employment in the rural economy. Cow dung would have a price in the village economy and bring some additional income to rural households. Methane which is generated from cow dung would get fully used for generating electricity. From a climate change perspective this would be a significant mitigation contribution by India; methane being a worse green house gas than carbon dioxide.

Poor management by municipal authorities of waste is an increasing health hazard. The primary reason for this has been the shortage of resources with the municipal bodies. Resource constraints are compounded by capacity constraints. Recovery from households of the actual costs of sewage treatment is just not feasible politically in the foreseeable future. Even full cost recovery of supply of drinking water as user charges is a daunting enough challenge. The other sources of income for municipal bodies are not rising fast enough. As a result the total quantity of untreated sewage is rising in the country as urbanisation grows. 100% treatment of all sewage needs to become a national goal with the highest priority. Similarly, untreated urban waste is rising across our cities. 100% modern treatment of solid waste must become a national goal of overriding priority. These goals would become feasible only if adequate resources are provided to the municipal bodies. Financial resource flows have to be combined with technical and management guidance and implementation conditions. These are essential given the enormity and complexity of the challenge. On health considerations alone these goals have a legitimate claim for priority in the allocation of resources with government. This can be done through direct central funding from the Swachh Bharat cess whose rates can be suitably increased if necessary. Alternatively, the Finance Commissions can earmark a large enough percentage of GST revenues to municipal bodies specifically for environment management. Only after resources are provided, does 100% treatment of sewage and 100% modern management of waste with segregation, recycling and conversion of waste to energy would become feasible.

Technological progress in waste water management has been quite significant in recent years. Decentralised bacterial treatment technologies for sewage treatment have made rapid strides. These are far cheaper. Long distance pipes are no longer required. Nor are large tracts of valuable land needed for traditional large sewage treatment plants which are still the norm for government agencies. Technical bureaucracies in public agencies have a real problem in India in adopting new technologies. They remain comfortable with their traditional technological specifications and tenders. Left to themselves they would continue doing more of the same. Central government leadership in prescribing processes and guiding technological modernisation would be a prerequisite for real progress in low cost efficient transition to 100% treatment. These decentralised bacteria based technologies are also ideal for settlements, urban slums as well as all villages, which are without sewage systems and where human waste makes its way through normal gravitational flows into the natural drainage system; from the small drains into the bigger ones and then into streams and finally rivers. This is the reason why repeated Ganga cleaning programs have not yet delivered, or, the Jamuna in Delhi is a big drain full of sewage and industrial effluents throughout the year except for a few weeks in the monsoons.

Urban solid waste management poses an even more complex set of issues and challenges. Western style segregation of waste at the household level is the ideal solution. However, the social reality of India with the kind of domestic help which middle class households are likely to have for the next decade makes household level segregation elusive. The hard reality is that effective segregation at the household level on a large scale is unlikely in the near future. Taking this reality into account, feasible measures for achieving effective segregation have to be attempted. Using the price signal creatively may work. There is a very large and efficient recycling network which works through persons (kabadiwallahs) who go to households and buy old newspapers, bottles and other items for which there is a good enough price in the market for them to recover their labour costs. To illustrate, they become the primary suppliers of old newspapers which becomes the raw material for the paper packaging industry. They even rummage through municipal waste bins in some places to see if they can find something of value. So one way forward would be to give them an attractive enough price for the waste which needs to be recycled, or, treated separately such as unusable electronic and electrical appliances, bulbs, metallic items and plastics. Once this system becomes effective enough in one compact area of a few apartment complexes, then the household waste, comprising primarily of kitchen waste, can, in theory, be treated in a decentralised manner in a closed container to get gas which can be used for electricity generation. This electricity may be more expensive but it should be mandatorily purchased by the local Distribution Company. The remaining solid would be compost which can be used as fertiliser. The other segregated wastes could then go to their respective modern recycling plants, or, waste treatment plants which would also need to be set up. These additional costs which would not be insignificant would also need to be borne fully from the Swachh Bharat cess.

If the principle of paying for waste which is not biodegradable and needs to be treated in a distinct manner works in some areas for some products, it can be extended gradually to cover all the plastic waste strewn across India. There is no other practical way of dealing with the plastic which is lying all over. Government agencies on their own would not be able to collect all the plastic.

Compliance with prescribed norms for industrial effluents has been a real challenge and the cause of considerable grass root resistance to the setting up of new industrial units. However, real time IT sensor based logging of the parameters of effluents simultaneously in the plant control room as well as in the Pollution Control Board should now be able to resolve the problem. If the norms are breached then the plant management should take a shut down and set things right. Failure to do so should attract severe pre determined escalating penalties from the Pollution Control Board. Such a sensor based monitoring system can be made fully operational in about eighteen months. Here the industrial units should be made to bear all the costs. These do not cost much and the individual industrial units can comfortably absorb the required costs. Such a system should fully take care of air and water pollution from the larger industrial plants. Solid waste from industrial units are, however, a relatively neglected area. There is the widespread practice of liberally permitting land use conversion for industrial units in the midst of rural areas. This has been a soft option due to the inability of the state to get new planned industrial areas developed rapidly enough to meet the full demand for affordable industrial land. This has been a mistake from an environmental perspective. Efficient environmentally benign management of industrial solid waste is far more economical in planned industrial areas than for industrial units spread across rural areas. These scattered industrial units need to be brought into a monitored system where their waste is collected and then treated in accordance with global best practices for recycling to the extent technologically and commercially viable and environmentally safe disposal for the rest. These units should pay the full costs for doing so in accordance with the polluter pays principle. This does not need any subsidy.

Then there are the vast number of medium, small and micro industrial units. These are in planned industrial areas, in the middle of older cities, in the slums and in unplanned unauthorised settlements on the outskirts. The challenge here is enormous. The essential first step would be an environmental audit, cluster by cluster, with respect to air, water, and solid waste generation. Then a diagnosis cluster by cluster of what is feasible and what the costs of mitigation measures would be. These units may not be able to absorb the full costs of technically feasible mitigation measures. There are good success stories of common effluent treatment plants, such as for chemical clusters in Vapi and textiles in Tirupur, with funding from the central government. These need to be replicated across all textile and chemical clusters in the first phase. In some cases, technological modernisation would not only reduce pollution but also improve competitiveness. Extending the gas grid to all industrial clusters in the country could result in the complete replacement of coal and oil for heating and other energy needs in industrial units. This would result in the elimination of air pollution from these units as gas is an energy source which does not pollute the air. This can be done in a commercially viable way as has already been done in some parts of India. This, again, does not need any subsidy. It has been needlessly delayed. There are other modernisation steps which may need some innovative financing, or, even some subsidies. A case by case industrial segment wise detailed assessment would be needed. Extreme sudden responses of mandating immediate closure, or, relocation are usually not sustainable.

For the measures suggested above, two basic principles are important. These are the benefits from competitive private sector participation and the advantages of quickly inducting globally cost effective technologies. The key for achieving both these objectives is repeated invitation of outcome based bids rather than process based bids. Typically, a government agency invites a bid for putting up a waste treatment facility by drawing up detailed specifications. After the facility is set up, the agency would manage the facility and incur operation and maintenance costs. What is being suggested is that bids be invited for setting up and running the facility with the bid parameter being the rate per unit of treating waste. The input and output parameters would have to be specified and a long term contract with minimum guaranteed supply of waste to be treated would be required. With the cost per unit conversion being the bid parameter and the choice of technology of conversion being left to the bidders, the best and most cost effective technologies would come in. The true life cycle cost would be reflected in the per unit treatment rate quoted. The problem of the technical bureaucracy's difficulty in going beyond inherited technical specifications would have been overcome. This principle could be applied to a common effluent treatment plant for a chemical cluster, or, to the management of electronic waste collected through the kabaddiwala supply chain. Successive bids across the country would get in the best technologies in a competitive industry structure for waste management across different segments in the country. As has been seen in other sectors, this should result in economies of scale and competition driving down costs substantially over time. The added advantage of this approach is that up front capital investment would be done by the private sector and government funds would be required only for paying per unit conversion charges. These should also be on a declining curve as more and more units are set up till the goal of 100% treatment is achieved. In an optimistic but not unrealistic scenario it may well turn out to be the case that actual annual costs for full treatment are far lower than may be estimated at the outset. However this involves a radical departure from the set ways of government agencies. Determined leadership from the central government who should impose this paradigm as a condition for central funding would be required. States and municipal bodies are now used to implementation conditions being part of central funding.

One key learning from other large and ambitious national programs has been that it is a good idea to begin with a large number of pilot projects in each identified area, go through the learning of getting the process and execution design right and only then begin scaling up. Initial success generates confidence and a momentum in favour of exponential growth.

India has the ability to undo the environmental deterioration that has occurred. It should begin doing so immediately. This is also affordable. With political commitment at all levels, a continuing process of consultation and consensus building, and use of the best talent available, a breakthrough is definitely possible within a few years. The people of India need a healthy environment at the earliest.

VIII

India@75: Vision for an Inclusive and Innovative Nation

– Chandrajit Banerjee

India is just five years from the milestone of celebrating 75 years as an independent nation. 1947 was a year of immense hope for the country when the country dreamed of regaining her historical wealth, splendor and vigor. As India embarked on her journey towards development, she had few resources and overwhelming challenges to overcome. Yet, against all odds and within constantly changing geopolitical and geo-economic environments, she sagaciously achieved notable progress. Today, as we approach 2022, all citizens are actively engaged in the endeavor of development and envisage a transformation of their fortunes.

In 1947, poverty alleviation was the major aspiration for the country and global leadership was the objective as India set forth on her journey of rejuvenation. The path has not always been easy, and the country has yet to complete the task of development. It is time for India to establish a new vision that will take her to unprecedented peaks of achievement.

India's advantages at this juncture in her development trajectory are impressive. Today, we are a young nation, as India experiences a bulge in her population pyramid in the age group of 15-34 years. With this cohort forming about 35% of the total population, India has a significant proportion of energetic, innovative and dynamic workers who can contribute to national development. It is widely expected that India will continue to experience growth in the total workforce for another two decades, which will be a key force driving savings, investments, and expansion of the national income.

Further, India has displayed technological aptitude that is far ahead of its position as a middle-income economy. The country has achieved impressive milestones such as the 'Chandrayaan' mission to the moon, multi-satellite launches, R&D engagement, science and technology progress, internet and mobile phone connectivity, startup culture and other trends which place her within a huge window of exciting opportunity. India's information technology (IT) sector contributes 7-9% of the GDP and leads in global exports of IT services. The internet user base is over 450 million, making it the second largest online market in the world after China. Mobile phone subscriptions have crossed the 1 billion mark, with smart phones being used by over 300 million persons. Such access to communication is an empowering feature of the country today.

India is also home to a vibrant entrepreneurial culture. 51 million micro, small and medium enterprises (MSME) are present across all corners of the country, contributing strongly to GDP, employment, manufacturing and exports. In addition, India has emerged as the world's third largest hub for technology startups after the US and UK, with almost 12,000 startups expected to come on stream by 2020.

It is time for India to maximize the opportunities in a strategic and visionary mode. There is need to create a new template for growth, a new matrix of interconnectedness as a nation, a new definition of the nation's future. It is time for India to emerge as the fastest growing economy for the next three decades, to win the battle over poverty decisively, and to provide the best possible lives for people across the country, whether in tiny hamlets in remote places or in huge mega polises.

VISION FOR INDIA@75

Inclusive development mandates that all citizens have equal access to the instruments that make their lives rich, productive and full of creativity. To do this, a collective vision for development and joint actions are required. The Confederation of Indian Industry (CII) actioned just such an agenda in 2008-09 under the rubric of its India@75 campaign. India at 75 is an in clusionary process that aims at redrawing and achieving the vision for India. Guided by Padma Bhushan Late Prof. C. K. Prahalad, India@75 undertook a pan-India campaign to articulate a shared vision which embraced a wide spectrum of society including students, farmers, policymakers, housewives, slum dwellers and so on. The vision document 'India@75—The People's Agenda' was evolved and encapsulates key parameters that Indian citizens across the country wish to action for themselves to attain goals they have set for 2022.

The discussion agenda for 2022 included the questions below:

- Can we have 500 million skilled workers?
- Can we have 100% literacy and 200 million qualified college graduates?
- Can we be home to 30 of the Fortune 100 firms of the world?
- Can we have 500 developed and smart cities?
- Can we be the preferred source of global innovation in technology and entrepreneurship?
- Can we have a national volunteer corps united in giving back to our motherland?

The India@75 program articulated the idea of a holistic three-dimensional development of India to acquire enough economic strength, technological vitality and moral leadership of the world. These and more are the overarching aspirations for India@75 and represent specific targets for where India would like to be 75 years after Independence in 2022.

The campaign has now moved from the visioning exercise to the action agenda, which has distilled the broad elements into several key areas of engagement. These in fact cover the major challenges that the country faces today and the agenda is directed at driving transformation in the identified areas. Since 2009, the vision has grown and dedicated efforts have led to internalization of the aspirations in many government policies now in place.

REFORMS PICK UP PACE

The distance between aspiration and achievements can be bridged through a concerted and collaborative effort if each citizen is aware of the potential and contributes to reach the targets. The Prime Minister referred to his dreams for India at 75 in his landmark speech at the US Congress in 2016, and it has been enshrined into the government campaign of Amrut Mahotsav announced by the Finance Minister in his Budget 2015-16 speech.

Amrut Mahotsav captures the targets of a roof for all or 20 million urban houses and 40 million rural houses, electricity in all households, road connectivity to each village, education institutions within 5 kilometers of every child, and affordable medical care. Livelihood generation and reduction of poverty are at the heart of the program, and visible changes in the lives of ordinary people are already taking shape as these elements are rolled out.

Within the troubled global environment since the global financial crisis, India has captured attention as the world's fastest growing large economy. India embarked on an economic reform journey 25 years ago, and a new generation has arisen ready to take on the world with its new capabilities. The reforms process has increased per capita incomes and dramatically reduced poverty. It has made India one of the most attractive destinations for global businesses.

In recent years, major reforms have transformed the economic landscape of the country. The Goods and Services Tax (GST) introduction in July 2017 makes India a single market for the first time. It is expected to simplify the business environment and make it easier to pay taxes. The GST Network places all taxpayers, central government and state governments on a single platform, able to register billions of transactions every month. The GST Council represents the best of a federal India, addressing GST matters in a quick and consensual mode.

Other major reforms include opening up of sectors to foreign direct investments, introduction of the Insolvency and Bankruptcy Code, lowering of corporate tax rates for new small manufacturing firms, and better administrative processes to enhance ease of doing business. These have resulted in concrete outcomes. The World Bank in its Doing Business Report 2018 placed India at rank 100, a huge jump of 42 positions in just three years. Ratings agencies have affirmed India's reforms process by raising its investment grade. FDI worth close to $195 billion has come into the country since April 2014, taking the total cumulative inflows to $518 billion by September 2017. Additionally, visible change is being made in creating infrastructure such as roads and highways, railways, ports and airports, and urban development.

TOWARDS 2022

India can attain a GDP growth rate of 9-10% that will alleviate poverty and provide a life of dignity to our citizens. It is estimated that this growth rate would need to be sustained over a period of two decades or more to bring the poverty head count ratio from the current 22% of the population to below 5%. In 2017, India had a total GDP of $2.4 trillion and a per capita GDP of $1,850 in real terms, translating into a GDP of $9.5 trillion and per capita GDP of $7,153 in purchasing power parity terms. Over the next five years to 2022, the economy is expected to grow at an increasingly faster pace ranging from 7.7% to 8.2%. This will take the GDP per capita in purchasing power parity terms to close to $11,000, according to estimates by the International Monetary Fund (IMF).

Technology will be the key enabler for achieving our vision of an inclusive and innovative nation. India is the fastest growing country for internet connections and Digital India is transforming our lives. India is making efforts to reach digital connectivity to each and every hamlet at the last mile. This technology can be leveraged for education and healthcare that will drive the productivity of our youth. Digital education and healthcare avenues can reach out to all and our mobile phones can become instruments of change.

Key force drivers that would need to be actioned in the next five years towards 2022 are outlined as below.

Education: A key pillar of India's future is education along with skill development. This will involve empowering our educational institutions at each level to surpass global benchmarks of excellence.

While the Right to Education Act bolstered by the Mid-Day Meal scheme has brought most children within the ambit of education, there are several challenges such as quality of education, drop-out rates at secondary level, and curriculum aligned to contemporary needs. For example, reading and maths achievement scores of children in class 5 are below 50%, while 127 million persons need to be trained by 2022.

Public expenditure on education must be increased to global norms of 6% of GDP from the current rate of 3.2%. One way of ensuring quality in schools is to encourage competition among them and permit parents to select their school of choice. Households may be provided with an educational grant through direct benefits transfer provided they send their children to school and achieve certain scores, similar to the system followed in Brazil. Better quality of teachers can be ensured through upgradation and modernization of teacher training institutes and their attendance should be mandated through biometric means. A model of merit scholarships can be used for lowering drop-out rates in secondary schools.

It is especially important to build technology usage in schools to create the right technological mindset among children. A special fund should be considered for providing infrastructure for this in schools across the country.

In addition, India must build the right institutions that will empower its people. World-class institutions of excellence, higher education, skill development and R&D institutes are required to enable youth to align to global developments. Currently, no Indian institution features in the list of top 100 global universities. At least 20 universities should strive to achieve global standards in humanities and sciences over the next five years.

The engagement of industry in education is significant and the sector is the most preferred for companies wishing to give back to society. Larger companies often run schools for workers and surrounding communities, while skill development is part of usual business practice. CII has undertaken specific programs to build industry engagement in universities and R&D institutes which includes funding doctorate studies, creating a platform for industry-academia linkages, and encouraging corporates to set up R&D centers in academic institutions.

Employment: Creating sufficient jobs and livelihoods for the working age demographics is an imperative and the foundations must be established in the coming five years so that by 2022, each young person is confident about their future in an inclusive country. New drivers of employment in a technology-enabled world can be envisaged. The shapes and sizes of enterprises will be critical as digital technologies enable micro-entrepreneurship, shared economies, and new platforms for generating livelihood. Growth of stronger enterprise clusters and networks of small enterprises will drive the new jobs.

To capture these opportunities, youth must have access to just-in-time, needs-aligned learning for creating the right skills. Re-skilling and upskilling in a modular format with skill capsules that enable workers to change sectors or shift to different types of work are the need of the hour. Further, linking urban and rural India through flows of natural produce can create more jobs. Urban India must emphasize the right transport and housing infrastructure that will promote leveraging agglomeration productivities, while rural India can benefit from non-agricultural economic activities.

The top ten job-creating sectors as per employment elasticity need special reform policies. These are identified as construction, services, healthcare, tourism, natural infrastructure and natural produce, education, transport and logistics, textiles and garments, manufacturing and retail.

Healthcare: A CII report estimates that using mobile phones for certain health delivery modules can save the country up to $1 billion in healthcare costs annually. This is a formidable saving, considering that non-communicable diseases alone can involve an expenditure of over $6 trillion between 2012 and 2030. Digital health can also be promoted through electronic health records which will lead to faster diagnosis and lower the cost of treatment. Telemedicine also lowers costs of consultation and connects remote regions. Big data, e-commerce in the pharma and clinic space and online registration systems are other forms of technology use in healthcare, which together can save India some $90 billion by 2035, and reduce the number of required hospital beds by over 1 million, according to another CII estimate.

Industry 4.0: With the technology-enabled industrial revolution shifting manufacturing and services sectors to a new level, India can assume a lead role in shaping the change. It can drive new product development, innovation and design, R&D and patents. The fourth Industrial Revolution, or Industry 4.0 as it is widely termed, involves multiple new technologies that are rapidly advancing, including Artificial Intelligence (AI), Machine Learning, the Internet of Things and 3-D printing. Services and software are increasingly embedded in products and are lowering human intervention, as more sophisticated machines are deployed in manufacturing units across the world.

The AI market in India is expected to grow at over 45% compound annual growth rate between 2016 and 2022. The country is believed to have three times the number of people working in tech-related roles in AI than China. Indian startups are already among the most dynamic and thriving in the world, converging technologies for new solutions. According to an article, new internet-savvy people from all income strata are overcoming illiteracy and using innovative apps developed by Indian entrepreneurs.

While progressive industry is doing its part in shaping the new revolution, as Industry 4.0 gathers pace, India should look at how to foster use of its different technologies in specific sectors including manufacturing, infrastructure, financial services, education, and so on. A deep analysis of the jobs that are at risk also needs to be conducted along with a mapping exercise of the new skill sets required to meet the challenges of emerging technologies.

Governance: In moral leadership, India stands as an exemplar with a vibrant model of democracy that allows its diversity to flourish. Tackling corruption and developing a responsive governance system is part of the vision for India at 75. Administrative reforms can make the governance process responsive, transparent and aligned to social needs, and make India a more efficient and productive economy. The next policy measures must include technology based administrative reforms. Corruption can also be addressed by infusing technology into administrative processes. There is a need to examine how simultaneous elections can be held for central and state governments in order to reduce administrative interruptions and ensure policy certainty.

Apart from these predominant strands, the effort for taking India to a new level by 2022 will involve several other proactive measures. India must build the right capabilities to manage urbanization. India will have 63 cities with a population of 1 million or more by 2025. Better urban management and right institutions to enable smooth transition are required so that there is adequate housing and transport rather than slums.

Another challenge is to ensure social security to all 500 million workers, including workers in both organized and unorganized sectors. The funds for this are possible from many different sources such as higher tax revenues, savings on subsidies through better management, insurance and pension schemes, and better savings instruments for households. Social security will enable flexibility to companies and make the Indian economy more efficient.

Women empowerment can add huge impetus to the Indian GDP. Currently, participation of women in the labour force at 27% is below global standards. To encourage women to come out to work, better policies will need to be designed for the workplace, while also ensuring their safety and security. Skilling at their place of residence, micro credit for productive purposes and boosting sectors with high women's participation such as textiles, healthcare, and education can help women to contribute to the national development agenda.

INDUSTRY INITIATIVES FOR INDIA IN 2022

Industry has come together under the India@75 mission to imagine a new India. The broad areas of the vision are being addressed in the themes of education and skill development; technology and innovation; agriculture and food security; business and economy; urbanization and environmental sustainability; arts, literature and sport; and moral leadership, governance and public administration.

CII's India@75 mission has established a range of initiatives to implement and leverage aspirations in this new environment. Flagship interventions are underway to enthuse and embrace more and more people and re-energize their interaction with the larger economy and society. The Power to Empower competition leverages the energy of entrepreneurship to capture new livelihood options. The Functional Literacy program for adults builds competencies among those who have missed out on schooling in their childhood. To promote technology and innovation capabilities, India@75 creates Hackathons which devise technology solutions for social development.

Our youth need to be more productive and the India@75 career counselling and job fairs build new linkages between academia and industry with youth as the connector agents. The India@75 National Volunteering Week in January brings together almost a million volunteers, ready to give their best to society. Pro Bono potential of corporate India is captured through capacity building and connecting with non-profit organizations. Finally, City Connect is a platform for new urban programs that directly benefit citizens. The platform today serves as the new engine to catapult India on its journey of change to 75 years as a free nation.

CONCLUSION

The task of strengthening India's inclusive development belongs to all sections of society, and industry has a special role to play in creating the new India. Industry has the responsibility of creating jobs and livelihoods, boosting innovation and R&D, promoting economic efficiency and productivity, integrating with the world, and ensuring sustainability of the development process. Collective action is the need of the hour and this can come from the right institutional processes and platforms to converge dispersed efforts. The government is playing a key role through a strong reforms process aimed at unleashing national entrepreneurship and easing the business environment.

Together, there is much that we can do to catapult India into the league of developed nations. India@75 is the next milestone, and the industry is prepared to address the challenges of national development as we head towards completing 75 years of our Independence as a nation.

IX

India in 2022: National Security Needs

– Lt. Gen. Satish Nambiar (Retd.)

Introduction

It would be presumptuous for analysts not privy to factual data regarding current equipment and ammunition holdings and operational plans of the Indian military, to profess to be able to make pronouncements on the actual state of preparedness with any degree of credibility. However, based on one's personal knowledge, past experience over the years, historical facts, attendance at various seminars, conferences, discussions, and so on that are regularly conducted, as also from the contents of official reports that are made public from time to time, it is possible to frame an analysis and make cogent observations on conceptual, functional, geo-political and organisational aspects that impact on the state of preparedness of the Indian military.

In doing so, it would only be fair to presume that the political and military leadership of the day will ensure that, within reasonable bounds of availability of resources for the purpose, and scope for acquisition from internal and external sources, essential requirements of trained manpower, weapons, equipment and ancillaries for the Indian Armed Forces, are provided for.

Civil-Military Relations

A major infirmity in the decision making apparatus pertaining to the evolution and oversight of India's security is the tenuous state of civil military relations. If the country's state of military preparedness is to be credible and effective, this must be set right without further delay. The malaise is rooted in the origins of our country as an independent country. The political leadership that assumed the reigns of governance from the British was never involved in addressing the security of the country; that was run from London. In fact, as it happened, on becoming independent, India's security policy was premised on non-violence and abhorrence of militarisation. Notwithstanding the fact that this premise was rudely shattered by the outbreak of hostilities and the prosecution of war in Jammu and Kashmir within months of attaining Independence, it took fifteen long years for the political leadership and the civilian bureaucracy to be shaken out of its self-induced stupor, when the Chinese launched military operations against us in October 1962.

Having been forced to come to terms with reality, the governing establishment took some tentative steps to redress the sorry state of affairs in the military, but even so, with a continuing deep distrust of the military as an institution, and an unforgivable lack of understanding of its vital role in the conduct of international relations. A comparison with the status of the military in the rest of the world at that time may be appropriate to place things in perspective for the analysis that follows. India gained Independence a couple of years after the end of World War 2; a war that lasted about six years; and followed only about 20 years after the equally, if not more, devastating experience of World War 1. Both wars had taken a huge toll in terms of loss of life and had severely impacted on the global economy. And before we forget, the contribution of the Indian military, albeit as a colony of Britain, was most significant in both wars. But an important fall-out of the two wars that has a bearing on the subject of this paper merits mention. In almost all democracies of the Western world, as also Communist countries like the Soviet Union, China and those in East Europe like Yugoslavia, large sections of the political leadership that emerged, both in governance and in opposition, had served in the military in one or both world wars. Even in the newly emerged independent nations like Indonesia, Egypt,

Cuba, Phillipines, South Korea, etc former military-men were at the helm of affairs. And of course, in our immediate neighbourhood, Pakistan and Burma fell to military dictatorship; in due course, Bangla Desh also briefly went down that path.

India was possibly the only major country in the world at that time where the political leadership, both in governance and in opposition, as also the civilian bureaucracy, had absolutely no war experience. In fact, they did not even have first-hand knowledge of matters military. While service in the military is no guarantee that relations between the governing establishment and the military will always run a smooth course, aspects like the deep distrust of the military that prevails, and not incorporating it in the evolution of security policy at the top level, are the outcome of this serious infirmity that is at the root of the sorry state of civil-military relations in our country. And we have paid dearly for it, as evident in the following instances: calling off military operations in Jammu and Kashmir in 1948 when poised for the capture of Muzaffarabad and most of what is now Pakistan Occupied Kashmir, without consulting the military; not acting on the well-considered advice of the military in so far as deployment on the borders with Tibet was concerned, as a consequence of which the debacle on 1962 ensued; not having senior military representation for consultation and advice during negotiations with Pakistan following the 1965 and 1971 wars; resulting in the return to Pakistan of strategic territory secured in Jammu and Kashmir in 1965, and surrendering at Shimla the fruits of the outstanding military victory secured in the Eastern theatre in 1971, that included about 93,000 Pakistani prisoners-of-war.

The unfortunate fall-out of the political leadership's distrust of the military and its consequent exclusion from top level deliberations is that the civilian bureaucracy and the intelligence establishment have found it expedient to interpose themselves between the military and the political leadership. Almost as if there is a need to interpret for the politician the viewpoint of the military. This is no doubt considerably facilitated by the closeness that develops between the civil service personnel and the police to the political class in the running of the administration, both at the Central Government and State Government level. Needless to say, the fact that significant sections of the civil administration and the police are more than prepared to do the bidding of their political masters adds to the comfort level of their mutual relationship. In marked contrast to the military whose tasks are reasonably well defined and cannot be compromised. To that extent, there is a perception in the military, and not without good reason, that the civilian bureaucracy has over the years used this proximity to the political class to steadily downgrade the status of the military and to ensure its continued exclusion from the decision making apparatus. This perception therefore has added to the slide in civil-military relations.

MILITARY AND DIPLOMACY

India's political leadership and civilian bureaucracy have been reluctant to recognise the contributions of its military to the making of the modern world and today's India. The Indian national movement was deeply divided in its attitudes toward the Indian Army under British rule. These divisions became sharper as the movement confronted the implications of World War II and the political choices it offered. While the Indian National Congress, speaking as the principal vehicle of the national movement, condemned the "imperialist war," individual leaders like Jawaharlal Nehru backed the Allied war effort against the fascists. Further accentuating the ambivalence within India's political leadership of the time, the "Indian National Army," led by Subhash Chandra Bose, used Japanese assistance in an effort to forcibly liberate India from the British. It was no surprise then, that the divided national movement could not leverage the Indian Army's extraordinary contribution to the Allied victory, in the negotiations with the British on the terms of independence, the distribution of the spoils of the war, and the construction of the post-World War 2 international order.

When India modified its economic orientation in the early 1990s and embarked on a liberalised and high-growth path, it put paid to its post World War II marginalisation in Asia and the Indian Ocean.

Given its size; geo-strategic location straddling the Indian Ocean; a population of over a billion people (and growing) with a demographic dividend in its favour; established democratic credentials; a significant capability in information technology; a large reservoir of scientific talent including in space technology; acknowledged management expertise; proven military capability; and the large market for consumer goods and services; an India that could produce an annual economic growth rate of 7-8 percent was bound to acquire the credentials for a engaging in vigorous regional diplomacy. Such rapid economic growth would easily provide for annual defence expenditures that would be large enough to modernise India's military capabilities.

The professionalism and competence of the Indian Armed Forces is recognised the world over. Some of our training institutions like the National Defence College in Delhi, the Defence Services Staff College in Wellington, the National Defence Academy in Khadakvasla, the Indian Military Academy in Dehra Dun, the Army, Navy and Air Force War Colleges, and so on, are outstanding by any standards; most countries including the developed ones, vie with each other to secure placements on the courses we run at these institutions. Our own officers deputed to attend courses of instruction at various levels at similar institutions abroad particularly in the developed world, have invariably been outstanding in their performance and drawn respect and praise; and developed long lasting relationships. We have over the years provided advice and expertise for setting up training institutions particularly in Africa; as in Ethiopia, Nigeria, Botswana, Uganda, etc. The contributions and performance of personnel and contingents of the Indian Armed Forces and civilian police in United Nations peacekeeping operations are the subject of praise and admiration by all, including by successive Secretary Generals and the UN Secretariat.

Given this established professionalism, expertise, and competence, there can be little discussion about the need to evolve an appropriate mechanism to synergise the political, diplomatic and military dimensions of India's foreign policy. Unfortunately, the sad irony today is that such synergy is conspicuous by its absence. Even within the Armed Forces there is little "jointness"; each Service believes it can win a war on its own. Between the Services and the Ministry of Defence, integration is a myth. It is no surprise therefore that there is no culture of a joint national approach between the different agencies of the Government. A large part of the blame lies with the political class for its lack of application towards both diplomacy as also matters military; and of course the 'turf' battles.

It is time we overcome the distrust, suspicion, envy and 'know it all' attitude that pervades the establishment. It is indeed sad that these non-issues are allowed to take precedence over national interests. Each agency has developed its own approach to address problems. It would appear that if synergy between the military and diplomacy is to be achieved there must be a method by which exchange of positions within the respective agencies is institutionally provided for. Senior military commanders have little or no experience of working with diplomats and vice versa. This needs to be remedied by providing for senior military representation in all diplomatic delegations and diplomatic representation in defence delegations.

MILITARY STRATEGY

In making observations about India's military strategy it is imperative to stress that the purpose is not to discuss operational plans. However, for purposes of this paper, an attempt is made to analyse some general aspects of our military strategy on the basis of information in the public domain and on the basis of operations conducted in the past. This is particularly relevant in context of some animated discussion in the public domain recently about the need for India's military to be prepared for the prosecution of a "two front war," "two and a half front war," etc. Made even more animated by the fact that the military hierarchy has itself engaged in pronouncements on the subject.

Before going any further, it is necessary to place the discussion in proper perspective. Is the discussion just about being able to "fight" on two, two-and-a-half, or three fronts? Or are we talking of prosecuting war on these fronts to bring it to a conclusion on terms that we have set for ourselves? Being clear about this is necessary in context of the fact that in all the conflicts that India has engaged in since attaining Independence in 1947, there is only one instance of the prosecution of war to a successful conclusion in military terms; the military operations that led to the defeat of the Pakistani forces and their unconditional surrender in the Eastern theatre in 1971, and the emergence of Bangla Desh as an independent country. It is another matter altogether, that the outstanding military achievements were squandered at the conference table in Shimla in 1972. In my view, because the political leadership either did not seek military advice, or found it appropriate to ignore such advice.

Even today, to the best of my knowledge, no matter against whom, simultaneously or otherwise, our operational plans envisage holding the adversarial forces at bay in areas where they have launched offensives, while prosecuting counter offensive operations in other selected areas, to secure some square kilometers of territory, to be used as bargaining chips at the negotiating table on termination of hostilities. This in my view, is fine, and can be dealt with on two fronts within our existing capabilities, if that is all our military strategic aims are about. However, I do think that for a country our size, and with the aspirations that we profess both economically and geo-politically, the bar must be set higher. And our capabilities developed accordingly.

Needless to say, all our political and diplomatic efforts must be directed at preventing war. But this does not always work and we may be forced into it, at which time we should not be found wanting in terms of capability or will.

In so far as Pakistan is concerned, should its political and/or military leadership provoke a war with us, our military aims should be to secure objectives and inflict unacceptable punishment on selected targets, that compel Pakistan to seek termination of hostilities on our terms; in Pakistan Occupied Kashmir, as also strategic objectives or targets in the hinterland; either to dismantle their politico-military command structure, or impact on politico-economic sustenance. There is no point engaging in 'half term' measures any longer.

As things stand, it does not appear that China would wish to engage in a conflict with India, as it does not serve its geo-political and economic interests to do so. As such, it would be prudent that we direct all our political and diplomatic efforts to prevent a war with the Chinese. But should that country seek to intervene in the event of a conflict with Pakistan, or should they initiate hostilities against India, our development of military capabilities, preparedness, and policy articulation, should be such as to convey the clear message that, not only will we defend our territory against attack by its forces, but use all our available capacity to inflict significant punishment against selected strategic targets in depth. And should Pakistan try to exploit such Chinese action, our operational response must be to inflict unbearable punishment on strategic objectives.

Needless to say, to enable the execution of such a military strategy, it is time we shed all rhetoric and bluster, and focus on developing the requisite capabilities and evolve operational plans accordingly. There is absolutely no need to articulate this in the public domain. I would venture to also suggest that it is time to review our declared nuclear doctrine in so far as "no-first-use" is concerned.

In the final analysis, it is important to remember that war and conflict are more than just equipment—they are tactics and training, leadership and morale, geography, logistics, and sometimes just plain luck. Technology alone does not win wars.

HIGHER DEFENCE ORGANISATION

The various measures discussed in preceding pages will, in my view, only bear fruit if the Higher Defence Organisation is radically restructured. The inadequacies and infirmities of the present structure of our higher defence organisation and the Ministry of Defence (that have been the subject of much discussion and comment in the years since Independence, but not acted upon) have been fully recognised, identified, and specific recommendations made at the senior political level for remedial action in the Group of Ministers report of February 2001, that made recommendations based on the report of the Kargil Review Committee. It is another matter altogether that, seventeen years on, while some action on a few recommendations of the report like the setting up of a Headquarters Integrated Defence Staff, the Andaman and Nicobar Command, and the Strategic Forces Command have been initiated, action on the more substantive aspects pertaining to the higher management of defence, such as the re-structuring of the Ministry of Defence and its integration with the Armed Forces Headquarters, appointment of a Chief of Defence Staff, and institutional measures for promotion of "jointness" between the three Services, have either not been pursued, or have been deliberately delayed by the machinations of a bureaucracy that has cleverly bypassed or ignored the directions of even the political establishment. It is indeed a telling reflection of the bankruptcy of our system that decisions taken by the political leadership are, where considered to their disadvantage by the bureaucratic machinery, referred for deliberation to bodies or committees constituted of members of the civilian bureaucracy or representatives decided upon by them, in order to either stymie implementation or delay the process indefinitely.

It is probably best to start the analysis of this theme by addressing the very first recommendation made by the GoM in para 6.14 of its report that states: "In order to give effect to this arrangement, the 'Transaction of Business Rules and Standing Orders' should be appropriately amended and issued." One is given to understand that these "Business Rules" that form the basis for the conduct of business by the Government of India are to be found in two volumes issued under the constitutional powers of the President of India in 1961. According to this set of rules, *"the responsibility for the defence of India, and every part thereof, including preparation for defence, and for the armed forces of the Union, namely Army, Navy and Air Force has been vested in the Defence Secretary."*

The most charitable explanation one can possibly put forward for such a ridiculous arrangement which would have been laughable had it not been not so serious, is that when the "Business Rules" were drafted soon after we proclaimed ourselves a Republic, those entrusted with the task, without doubt from the civil services, would have, as is more often than not the case, got hold of our colonial masters' documents on the subject, and gone about doing a "cut and paste" job to fit what they would have considered were our requirements. It is therefore more than likely that the portion on the responsibility for the defence of the country would have been copied verbatim from the British document. Not allowing for the fact (deliberately or otherwise), that in the British system, then as is even now, the 'Defence Secretary' is a political appointee, a member of the cabinet nominated by the Prime Minister to hold the charge of the defence portfolio, and not the senior-most civilian bureaucrat, who in the British system is the permanent under secretary for defence. In our case, the provisions in the draft would have served our civilian bureaucracy well in terms of denying the military leadership in the persons of the Commanders-in-Chief or later the Chiefs of Staff, a role in government. Whether the political leadership of the time or even the military leadership, saw through the fallacy of the arrangement, can only be a matter of conjecture. However the important point at issue is, that in so far as one can ascertain, no attempt has been made to implement this first and most important recommendation given in the GoM report of 2001. It is therefore time that we put in place an institutionalised arrangement that ensures that the responsibility for the defence of the country is vested, not in the civilian bureaucracy, but in the political leadership, represented in our case by the Defence Minister, with the assistance of a Chief of Defence Staff (when that appointment is made) and the Service Chiefs, and through him to the Cabinet Committee on Security headed by the Prime Minister. To that end, steps should be taken without any further delay to amend the Government Business Rules to the effect that *"the responsibility for the defence of India, and every part thereof, including preparation for defence, and for the armed forces of the Union, namely Army, Navy and Air Force is vested in the Defence Minister (Raksha Mantri)."*

Restructuring of the Ministry of Defence really implies review of its manning policies to ensure that there is in-built capacity for understanding operational commitments, equipment requirements, and administrative needs of the Armed Forces. With all the right intentions, the current arrangement of generalist IAS officers moving into the Ministry and back to their state cadres, or out to other central government ministries, is barely workable, leading to periodic tensions in relations between the military and the civilian components. Not quite the arrangement for such a vital organisation responsible for the security of the nation. Regrettably, what has been done in the last seventeen years since the release of the GoM report has been largely cosmetic and most unconvincing.

The best arrangement for manning the Ministry of Defence is without doubt having civil service officers from a dedicated national security cadre, who could move around within the security apparatus at the central government including within the Home Ministry, as also to similar offices at state government level. Obviously supplemented and complemented by induction of officers from the two organisations so closely involved with the evolution of policies on national security and their implementation, the Armed Forces and the Foreign Service.

The need to have a Chief of Defence Staff within the Indian higher defence structure has been the subject of discussion in earlier years from time to time without any real moves towards fruition. However, the Kargil Review Committee and GoM reports have quite categorically asserted that it is time for the institution of this office together with a Vice Chief of Defence Staff and an integrated headquarters in order to provide single point military advice to the Government, exercise control over India's strategic forces, enhance the efficiency and effectiveness of the planning process through intra and inter Service prioritisation, and promote required jointness in the Armed Forces. It is indeed a matter of some irony that despite the recommendations of the GoM and the prodding of the Standing Committee on Defence, there has been no progress on this issue.

This is a decision to be taken by the political leadership on its own merit. It is indeed unfortunate and a sad reflection of the knowledge of matters military, and the capacity for taking decisions, that despite the recommendations made by the Group of Ministers in their report, successive Governments have not been able to muster the will to 'bite the bullet' as it were. To the best of one's knowledge, the reasons put forward for not being able to arrive at a decision is the lack of consensus within the three Services. This is a contention that needs to be placed in the right perspective. In the last few decades, nowhere in the world has such an arrangement been put in place with the agreement and consensus of the various components of the armed forces. The decision has, in every case, been taken by the political authorities, and implementation ordered through acts of Parliament. The service chiefs were directed to implement the decision and do so without question, even where they were not necessarily fully in agreement with it. Those in the military hierarchy who felt strongly enough about their disagreement with the political decision, were allowed to leave with grace and dignity, and enable implementation by others down the line.

There is absolutely no difference of opinion within the Armed Forces, other sections of the governing establishment, and the strategic community, that 'jointness' and 'integration' are key to success in operations in the emerging environment. The debate really appears to be only on how this is best achieved. The arrangements that served us in the past, not always to the desired degree, are just not robust or resilient enough to deal with the rigorous demands that will be placed on our security apparatus in the foreseeable future. In context of the changes that have, and are, taking place at the geo-strategic plane, and the possible demands that we are likely to be faced with, it is no longer possible for single service chiefs to oversee the conduct of operations.

There is therefore little doubt that if we are to undertake future operational commitments effectively, as important as the case for the creation of the post of a "Chief of the Defence Staff," is the compelling requirement for divesting the Service Chiefs of the responsibility for the oversight and conduct of land and air operations on our Western, North-Western, Northern and North-Eastern borders, as also air and maritime operations off our Eastern and Western sea-boards and beyond, by the establishment of "Theatre Commands." Theatre commanders would then be directly responsible on operational matters to the Defence Minister and the Cabinet Committee on Security through the Chief of the Defence Staff. Such an arrangement cannot and should not be put off any longer. Simultaneously, in context of the fact that allocations for defence needs will invariably impose considerable strain on national resources and therefore be more and more difficult to come by, every effort must be made to save on avoidable expenditure. To that end it is imperative that we take immediate measures to remove duplication and triplication of personnel requirements and infrastructure on training and logistics, by pooling the resources of all three Services, and maybe even of para-military organisations like the Coast Guard, to a common joint Services grid. In order to manage such an arrangement it would be appropriate to also set up "Functional Commands" that complement the "Theatre Command" concept.

Directives to theatre commanders for the planning and conduct of operations within the framework of a National Security Strategy approved by the National Security Council should be provided by the Cabinet Committee on Security through the Defence Minister and the Chief of Defence Staff (CDS). Apex level operational control over theatre commands would also be best exercised by the Cabinet Committee on Security through the Defence Minister and CDS.

X

Indo-US Relations

– Prof. Chintamani Mahapatra

To visualize the next five years of relations between India and the United States, one needs to examine the shape, nature and quality of India's ties with the US during at least last five years. And that means the overall developments in Indo-US relations during the second term of the Obama Administration.

It is important to recall that when Barack Obama won the 2008 US presidential elections, questions were raised in India and the United States about the continuity of a bilateral strategic partnership that was evolving since the closing years of the Clinton Presidency and that had considerably matured under the eight years of the George W Bush years in the White House.

While India's defense and security ties, involving periodic military exercises, rising defense trade, sharing of intelligence and counter terrorism cooperation, had intensified by the years under the Bush Presidency, the most significant development that altered the paradigm of India's engagement with the United States was the signing of the civil nuclear cooperation agreement. India was the target of the US-led international non-proliferationregime for about three decades and President George W Bush liberated India from that nuclear technology control regime by signing a civil nuclear cooperation agreement.

This agreement was the result of years of painstaking official negotiations and public debate and diverse international reactions. When Obama won the presidential election, doubts were raised about implementation of the US-India nuclear deal. During the election campaign, presidential hopefuls Barack Obama and Hillary Clinton championed the cause of nuclear and missile non-proliferation. When Obama became the US President and appointed Hillary Clinton as the Secretary of State, apprehensions were raised that CTBT and NPT would return to haunt the US approach towards India. It was feared that putting NPT and CTBT in the foreign policy priority of the Obama Administration would create hurdle in the implementation of the nuclear cooperation agreement.

For the first few months of the new Obama Administration, India did not bleep in the Obama's foreign policy radar confirming the apprehension regarding the non-proliferation front. It was clear that any derailment of the 123 Agreement on nuclear cooperation would have adverse effect on the emerging trajectory of bilateral strategic partnership. Hillary Clinton, the US Secretary of State, visited a host of Asian countries to underline the attention Obama White House would put on the country's relationship with the Asian countries. India was not part of her itinerary!

However, when Secretary Clinton visited India in July 2009, all speculations and anxiety related to Washington's position on non-proliferation issues vis-à-vis India was set at rest. She made a clear announcement that NPT/CTBT would not come on the way of implementation of the 123 nuclear Agreement. Soon political, diplomatic, economic and security aspects of India-US relations assumed an upward trajectory. Barack Obama became the first US President to visit India during his first term in office. Speaking on the floor of the Indian Parliament Obama described India as an "emergent power" in world affairs, unlike the usual description of India as an "emerging power" by many leaders and scholars. Going above his predecessor's policy of removing India from the target list of the non-proliferation regime, Obama assured his support to make India a member of all kinds of non-proliferation regimes. He went a step further in declaring his resolve to support India's candidature to become a permanent member of the UN Security Council.

During the Obama Administration's first term the US relations with India reached new heights. Military exercises held jointly by

Indian and American armed forces, defense technology trade made easy by the Pentagon, counter-terrorism cooperation given a boost by the appropriate agencies of the two countries, enhanced trade and mutual foreign investments and good political chemistry between the Indian and American leadership, Obama's efforts to combat the Taliban and Haqqani forces, his attempt to reign in Islamabad's selective cooperation in counterterrorism measures and several other factors made it appear as if the emerging strategic partnership between India and the United States had become rock-solid.

However, the Devyani Khobragade episode rang the alarm bell that one single event could derail decades of constructive works to build a comprehensive strategic partnership between India and the United States. Washington's slow and lackluster initiatives to resolve the issue and the heightened emotional reaction in India against the arrest and humiliation of a lady Indian diplomat threatened the continuity of the strategic partnership. In a way this was a wake up call to both Washington and New Delhi. While during the course of building up the strategic partnership under the new context of post-Cold War era it was often repeated that no single issue would or should affect the bilateral relationship, the Khobragade episode exemplified the unforeseen single issue that could turn the relationship bitter. This serves as a pointer when one tries to peep into the future of Indo-US relations!

Prospects of India's relations with the United States did not look bright when the BJP won the national parliamentary elections in May 2014 under the dynamic leadership of Narendra Modi. The main apprehension revolved around the fact that Modi had been denied visa to visit the US by successive US administrations for about nine years. When Narendra Modi became the Indian Prime Minister the momentum in Indo-US relationship had considerably slowed down not only because of the diplomatic standoff mentioned above but also because of developments in India that had made the central government literally dysfunctional. Series of corruption and scandals reported in the media had tarnished the image of the leadership and the country. Lack of adequate economic reforms, according to American analysts and observers, had discouraged the US trade and business sectors from focusing on Indian market. Questions were raised about the longevity and the strength of the strategic partnership. Could rise of Modi accelerate the decline of Indo-US strategic relations? Could Obama's stated ambition to end the US military operations embolden Pakistan to re-energize its policy of sponsoring anti-India terrorist activities? Could India handle the Chinese assertiveness and Pakistani belligerence in the midst of a declining trend in the momentum of Indo-US strategic ties?

There is little doubt that all these apprehensions disappeared when Prime Minister Narendra Modi promptly expressed his willingness to visit the United States at the invitation of President Barack Obama. Modi's first visit to the United States, contrary to expectations, was a grand success. He quickly established a positive chemistry with President Barack Obama. Since then the number of times the Indian Prime Minister and the American President met was unprecedented and exemplified the importance attached to India by Washington and the priority New Delhi allotted to its foreign and national security policy.

Three key aspects of Indo-US relations under the Modi government and the Obama Administration are: a broad consensus over building cooperation in handling Pakistan/Afghanistan/terrorism conundrum; managing the muscular foreign policy of China and strengthening institutions and agencies that are part of defense and security matrix. Consequently, Washington no longer refrained from condemning Pakistan's cross-border terrorist activities; India came more openly against Chinese assertiveness in South China Sea and elsewhere; and India continued to expand its constructive activities with persistent Pakistani opposition and indirect US support. In addition, India's relationship with Iran was not allowed to derail Indo-US strategic consensus, despite high-pitch US rhetoric and biting sanctions against Iran. By the time, President Obama exited the Oval Office, defense technology and trade partnership had matured and special arrangement had been made in the Pentagon to bypass bureaucratic delays in transfer of high defense technology to India.

Both Narendra Modi and Barack Obama had witnessed how Indo-US ties were stable and cooperative in the midst of rising US-Pakistan tension and Sino-US mistrust. Obama's exit strategy to end US military presence in Afghanistan and inability to effectively Chinese military fortification of islands and reclaimed islands in South China Sea had raised concerns in the Indian mind. But the real blow to stability in Indo-US relations came when Donald Trump became the US President. Trump's unpredictability generated unprecedented level of disquiet in domestic political processes and high level of unease among the US allies as well as foes in the international community. His unconventional methods of diplomacy, abrupt reactions to world events and opposition to traditional pattern of US foreign and defense policy raised several questions about the future of Indo-US relations.

President Trump raised questions over relevance of NATO, demanded more financial contributions from allies, asked Japan and South Korea to defend themselves, if need be by making their own nuclear weapons; walked out of the Trans-Pacific Partnership (TPP) negotiations; proposed renegotiation of North American Free Trade Agreement (NAFTA), suspended assistance to Pakistan on terrorism related concerns, did not back Trans Atlantic Trade and Investment Partnership (TTIP); threatened a trade war with China, declared an "America First" economic policy and took many more such steps that made deciphering his approach towards India very difficult.

Thus when Prime Minister Narendra Modi visited Washington to have the first summit with President Donald Trump, no one had any clue about the possible outcome of this summit. British Prime Minister, German Chancellor and many other world leaders reportedly did not receive expected "welcome" from the Trump White House. Many analysts also raised questions about the compatibility of Modi's "Make in India" policy and Trump's "American First" policy. Some argued that Trump's anti-China rhetoric had given way to American pragmatism when Chinese President Xi Jinping visited the US. China was no longer dubbed as a currency manipulator and the US was fully ready to continue its trade and investment ties with

China. If Trump had bought the Chinese theory of a "new kind of great power relationship," what would be the fate of India-US strategic partnership? Would Trump come hard on Pakistan, especially against Islamabad's anti-India activities, despite his policy to continue the war in Afghanistan?

However, the outcome of Modi-Trump summit was unexpectedly positive. The strategic partnership project did not face any major challenge. The defense and technology trade initiative also survived. Military to military cooperation would go ahead. It was also made clear that differences would have to be sorted out on a host of economic issues, including the visa fee issue, HIB visa issue, bilateral investment treaty negotiations and market opening issues.

One of the key developments in Indo-US relations under the Modi government and Trump Presidency is growing significance of the "Indo-Pacific" strategic concept. The National Security Strategy Report issued by the Trump White House has made it clear that instead of "Asia Rebalancing," the US would focus on peace, stability and development in the larger Indo-Pacific region. India has a prominent role to play in this strategic scheme. The US for long has been pushing India to play the role of an important security provider in the Indian Ocean region. The Modi Government has declared that India is a security provider in the Indian Ocean. But the aspiration is to enlarge the area to encompass the entire Indo-Pacific region!

While Indian navy is not yet in a position to play such a role beyond the Indian Ocean region, developments in South China Sea and East China Sea where China's assertiveness is threatening the stability of the regions have drawn Indian attention. India, unlike in earlier times, has openly taken a position and has called for "freedom of navigation" and respect for law of the sea. India has energy and trade interests in the region and has expressed concerns over the continuing disputes over sovereignty. Indo-US joint statements have included concerns over South China Sea developments and are reflective of growing strategic consensus and common visions on security threats. Besides, the restoration of the Quadrilateral initiative involving naval cooperation among India, Australia, Japan and the United States is a bold step in the direction of consolidating Indo-US naval cooperation.

CHALLENGES IN NEXT FIVE YEARS

The following challenges will confront India and the United States in coming years. First of all, there will be national elections in India in 2019 and presidential elections in the United States 2020. Will Narendra Modi's party return to power in next election? Will there be a change in Indo-US relations if another party/parties form government in New Delhi? There is a broad consensus now across the political spectrum in India to continue with the country's strategic partnership with the United States. There is no chance of any future government in India walking away from the current policy vis-à-vis the United States. However, the internal political equations, pace of economic reforms, degree of resolve and modalities adopted by a future government to face the challenges across the Indo-Pakistan and Sino-Indian borders will have an impact on India-US relations.

Likewise, Donald Trump's reelection will provide continuity to US strategic ties with India. The second term of Trump will witness further strengthening of the administration's policies, which at the moment appears stronger on defense and security sectors and problematic in economic and social sectors. If a Democratic candidate wins the 2020 presidential election, it would be most likely a return to the days of Obama years.

There are differences between India and the United States on a host of economic and social issues that would continue to drive the relationship. The US, for instance, would continue to push for more and more market opening in India and the Indian government would have to strategize to protect Indian interests, particularly sectors affecting the Indian farmers, labour class and to certain extent small and medium scale industries. The Indian American community serves as a social bridge between the two countries when the American economy performs well and the contribution of Indians in the US draw appreciation and praise. But at the time of economic stress, the administrations, such as Trump's, would adopt policies that would disrupt socio-cultural cooperation between the two countries. Such disruptions would not derail the comprehensive ties between the two countries, but would certainly constitute periodic irritants.

Second important challenge to Indo-US ties would come from developments in Afghanistan and along India-Pakistani borders. Will the Afghan war continue for next five years? Will Trump begin to negotiate a way out of the Afghan imbroglio? How much importance will the Trump Administration give to India's role in the exit strategy, if any, will certainly shape the depth of Indo-US counter terrorism collaborations. The challenge for Indian diplomacy would be to carve a place for itself in the loop that would determine the future course of US action in Afghanistan. Is there a possibility of a sudden or speedy withdrawal of US forces from Afghanistan? There is no doubt that India's interests will have least priority for the US administration while charting out and implementing an exit strategy and thus challenge for India would be to guard against it and begin to war game on this scenario.

The future of US-Pakistan relations in this context will certainly influence the course of Indo-US relations. Will the US come hard on Islamabad as it did in late 1980s and early 1990s? Will that further consolidate Sino-Pakistan strategic collaborations? Will China be unable to play the role the US did in Pakistan? Alternatively, will Pakistan be more vulnerable to China's influence in the absence of US influence? How can India handle a scenario where there is no credible US influence over Pakistan?

Third, important development that has been simmering for years now and will most likely intensify in coming years is a sort of Cold Confrontation" between the United States and China. It was the US that was responsible for making China alter its course of economic policy and embark on a path of export-led growth strategy that has today brought enormous wealth and strength to that country. But for the US efforts to open China, make it a counterweight to the former Soviet Union, help its economic expansion by offering it a huge market and making its allies follow similar approach towards China, the history of China's evolution would have been qualitatively different. But that policy has brought huge dividend to China making it the second largest economy in the world and third largest military power in the globe.

But the significant consequence of it is today's Cold Confrontation between the sole superpower and an aspirant superpower. The economic interdependence between the US and China and political competition between the two for global influence make it difficult for them to wage Cold War against each other but make it harder for them to avoid cold confrontation. The Sino-US tension in the South China Sea and East China Sea, the apparent Chinese goal to establish its hegemony in the Indo-Pacific and the US efforts to subtly counter that, and the dilemma faced by US allies and strategic partners to take positions on issues of Sino-US differences are some of the characteristic features of the Col Confrontation.

This is precisely what is going to affect India's foreign policy choices in coming years. During the Cold War era neither the United States nor China was strategically comfortable with India's rise. In the post-Cold War scenario, India has sought to maintain and enhance comprehensive strategic partnership with the United States and simultaneously has tried to give a positive boost to its economic, social and cultural relations with China, despite Beijing's unhelpful attitude towards the territorial disputes and unsafe cooperation with Pakistan to the extent of shielding Islamabad's "dirty tricks" department and terrorist-sponsoring activities.

As the Cold Confrontation unfolds and China increasingly views Indo-US defense and security collaborations as one of the anti-China mechanisms of the United States, India's diplomacy would face periodic challenges. Indian analysts repeatedly state that India does not support any anti-China strategy. Indian Government is admittedly opposed to the idea of "Containment of China," but the Chinese analysts have a different take. There are votaries in the US policymaking and policy analysis circles who view Indo-US strategic partnership as a bullwark against Chinese assertiveness and such views further encourage the Chinese apprehensions over Indo-US strategic cooperation. But the big challenge before the government of India would be to deftly navigate in the waters of Sino-US Cold Confrontation. Will the US take position on Sino-Indian territorial disputes? The answer is a big "No." Will the US side with the US in the case of any future India-China War? There is no certainty at all, in the absence of a mutual defense treaty. Can India handle the growing Chinese assertiveness and often misbehavior or misadventure in India's strategic environment? The answer is again a big "No." Can India be assured of political support of its neighbours on issues related to Sino-Indian differences? Again, China has successfully expanded its influence in the decision-making bodies of most of India's neighbouring countries by using its foreign aid diplomacy and India's resources are very limited compared to that of China? Will then India's comprehensive strategic partnership be of utmost relevance in this context? It needs strategic analysis.

Last, but not least, increasing US-Russian tension too will be a determinant in future Indo-US relations. Russia seems to be back as a great power in international affairs. The US has remained completely helpless or has acted as bystander when Moscow began to assert its position in the affairs of Caucasus, Baltic Republics, Ukraine, Central Asia and other parts of the former Soviet space. Russia's influential role in the Middle East too is visible. European dependence on Russian energy is a factor that has already complicated Trans-Atlantic strategic equations. NATO has survived and expanded in the post-Cold War era. Yet, its ability to handle Russian role has diminished in view of Moscow's ability to expand its relationship with US allies and showcase its enormous military prowess.

Russia's unhappiness over its shrinking arms market in India is not hidden. While Indo-Russian economic ties and trade cooperation is miniscule compared to India-US economic ties, Russia has over the decades proved to be a reliable partner—a tag not fully applicable to India's ties with the United States. Given the continuing relevance India's strategic cooperation with Russia, present and future tension in US-Russian relations will bring thought-provoking questions for Indian foreign policy establishment.

The mantra that guides Indian foreign policy makers is "strategic autonomy." Perhaps, this guiding principle has led India to participate in a triangular mechanism with Russia and China-Russia-China-India Triangle. It is this principle that guides India's participation in BRICS, where Russia and China are very much part of the grouping. But, simultaneously, it is the same principle that encourages India to shape a Quadrilateral Grouping along with the United States, Japan and Australia. All these groupings are work in progress and all have faced ups and downs. Is it India's smart non-alignment? If so, it actually sets the boundary of Indo-US strategic partnership. In coming years, one cannot expect emergence of any Indo-US strategic alliance. One cannot expect a trouble free Indo-US strategic partnership, no matter who occupies the Oval Office in Washington, DC. India's experiment with strategic autonomy is a goal worth seeking, yet in an interdependent world the limits of "autonomy" need to be delimited. And this is where the strategic thinkers and policy planners in India need to put their mind together.

XI

National Security: Meeting Future Threats and Challenges

– Brig Gurmeet Kanwal (Retd)

ABSTRACT

The unstable regional security environment in southern Asia has vitiated the atmosphere for socio-economic development and the alleviation of poverty. The foremost cause of continuing instability is the ongoing conflict in Afghanistan and along the Afghanistan-Pakistan border. Unresolved territorial and boundary disputes with China and Pakistan, neither of which is close to resolution, and the nuclear warhead-ballistic missile-military hardware nexus between the two countries, carry the seeds of possible future conflict that may present a two-front situation to India. As both of India's military adversaries are nuclear-armed, India's future wars will be fought under the nuclear shadow. Pakistan's proxy war in Jammu and Kashmir and Pakistan-sponsored urban terrorism in other parts of India, remnants of the insurgencies in the north-eastern states and the threat of Left Wing Extremism across large tracts of central India loom large on the country's strategic horizon and contribute markedly to instability. The efforts being made by the Government of India to speedily resolve internal conflicts have not yet been successful except that a cease-fire with the Nagas held up for over ten years before one faction walked out and the ULFA in Assam has recently agreed to negotiate with the government. India needs to formulate a comprehensive national security strategy, undertake military modernisation in earnest and upgrade its combat capabilities in order to successfully face emerging threats and challenges. The present defence budget, which is less than 1.60 per cent as a ratio of the projected GDP, is grossly inadequate to meet the requirement.

Regional Security Environment

India is an ancient civilisation, but a young nation state that is still engaged in the process of nation building. As an emerging regional power, India's national security environment is influenced by developments at the global and regional levels and, since the turn of the century, the news has not been very encouraging. The polycentric new world order, which had begun to emerge gradually from the ashes of the Cold War, is now fraying at the edges. The primary causes for this situation are the growing friction among the major powers, the triumphant rise of ultra-right wing political parties, dilution in the forces of globalisation and free market economies and the world's failure to comprehensively defeat the Islamic State.

While the progress made in liberating Mosul, Aleppo and Raqqa has forced the Caliphate to retreat from most of the areas that it had captured during its triumphant march across Syria and Iraq, its virulent ideology continues to flourish unabated. In fact, a cyber caliphate is gradually coalescing. This manifestation of the Caliphate will be more dangerous than its geographical counterpart due to the ability to exploit the Internet to radicalise vulnerable youth all over the world. Elsewhere in West Asia, the Arab-Israeli conflict continues to linger on with Iran playing spoiler in the peace process, the Kurds stepping up their fight for an independent homeland and Shia-Sunni tensions further exacerbating the volatile situation. Unless Russia and the United States (US) stop competing for influence and join hands with the rest of the international community to resolve the multifarious challenges afflicting the region, peace and stability will remain elusive in West Asia.

The nuclear deal that Iran signed with the US, giving up its ambition to acquire nuclear weapons, was arguably the most significant foreign policy achievement of the US since the Camp

David accords of 1978. The deal has held up despite the advent of the Trump administration in January 2017 and continuing opposition from several regional neighbours of Iran like Israel and Saudi Arabia. Whether the nuclear deal will survive in the long-term is still uncertain. However, if it is abrogated by either signatory, the world will surely witness the arrival of another nuclear power–with attendant consequences. Iran's nuclear weapons are unlikely to be acceptable to the Trump administration or Prime Minister Netanyahu or to the Saudis.

Forgotten in the shadow of the conflict in Syria and Iraq is the civil war in Yemen. The Houthis and their allies, who seized Sanaa in September 2014, are locked in a bitter fight with a Saudi-led coalition comprising mainly Arab nations from the Gulf. General Raheel Sharif, who retired in November 2016 as Pakistan's army chief, is heading the Saudi-led 34-nation coalition that has been assembled to fight Islamist terrorist groups.

The unstable security environment in Afghanistan and along the Afghanistan-Pakistan border is the greatest cause of instability in southern Asia. The present situation in Afghanistan can be described as a strategic stalemate between the Afghan government and the remnants of the NATO forces on one side and the Taliban and Pakistan-sponsored terrorist organisations like the Haqqani network on the other. While speaking during the Heart of Asia conference at Amritsar in December 2016, President Ashraf Ghani had snubbed Pakistan's offer to invest US$ 500 million for the reconstruction of his war-torn country. Indicting Pakistan in severe terms, he said the Taliban insurgency would not survive even one month if it did not get sanctuary in Pakistan and support from it.

Announcing his country's commitment to staying the course in Afghanistan, US President Donald Trump put Pakistan on notice for encouraging terrorist organisations to destabilise neighbouring countries. Attempts at reconciliation and carrying forward the peace process have made no headway. The Taliban as once again showing signs of resurgence and, if the Afghan National Army fails to neutralise it quickly with NATO support, the situation may degenerate in to a civil war in three to five years. Meanwhile, the strategic stalemate is likely to endure.

China's growing nuclear warhead-ballistic missile-military hardware collusion with Pakistan and the two countries' unresolved territorial disputes with India together pose a formidable national security threat to India. Despite misgivings in both countries, the China-Pakistan economic corridor (CPEC) has begun to take shape. Passing through Gilgit-Baltistan in Pakistan occupied Jammu and Kashmir (PoJK), the US$54 billion CPEC project will link Xingjian province of China with Gwadar on the Makran coast west of Karachi. Though Pakistan is raising a division of approximately 12,000 personnel to provide security for the CPEC against terrorist attacks, eventually Chinese soldiers are bound to be inducted for this purpose just like has happened earlier in Gilgit-Baltistan. The large-scale presence of PLA personnel on Pakistani soil will further vitiate the security environment.

Surprisingly from India's point of view, India's long-time strategic partner, Russia, has expressed its support for CPEC. Russia also held a low-level military exercise with Pakistan and has offered to sell arms to the country. These developments are detrimental to India interests and could to some extent be attributed to the Obama administration's policies that drove Russia closer to China.

Internal instability continues to haunt the government of Pakistan and its army. Two years and three summers after it was launched, Operation Zarb-e-Azb in Khyber-Pakhtoonkhwa is still to be concluded successfully. A low-grade insurgency in Balochistan, unrest in Sind and Gilgit-Baltistan, creeping Talibanisation, ethnic tensions and a weak economy are a potent mix that could lead to an implosion.

India's red lines have been repeatedly crossed by state-sponsored Pakistani terrorists in recent years. In September 2016, after an attack on a military camp at Uri, India conducted surgical strikes over a broad front across the LoC and also launched targeted fire assaults. India is likely to continue to inflict punishment on the Pakistan army for every act of terrorism planned and directed by the ISI. India has suspended bilateral negotiations with Pakistan. Its new policy may be described as tactical assertiveness under the umbrella of strategic restraint as war with Pakistan is not in India's interest.

Simmering discontentment in Tibet and Xinjiang against China's repressive regime is gathering momentum and could result in an open revolt. Varying degrees of turmoil in other countries around India, including Bangladesh, Maldives, Myanmar, Nepal and Sri Lanka, also contributes to regional instability. Narco-terrorism, the proliferation of small arms, the circulation of fake currency, trans-border money laundering and the availability of sanctuaries for insurgents, often aided and abetted by neighbouring states, enable non-state entities to challenge duly elected governments. The insurgent movements in India's north-eastern states are an example of this phenomenon.

The prevalence of volatility in the region leads to the inevitable conclusion that southern Asia will continue to remain unstable for some more time to come. The countries of the region must come together in their own interest and agree to systematically plug the loopholes that enable cross-border insurgent movements to flourish. However, there is too much mistrust among the neighbours. Also, with SAARC now almost completely defunct, nor is a viable umbrella available to enable the conduct of long and hard negotiations that would be required.

India's standing as a regional power that has global power ambitions and aspires to a permanent seat on the UN Security Council has been seriously compromised by its inability to successfully manage ongoing conflicts in its neighbourhood, singly or in concert with its strategic partners. These conflicts are undermining southern Asia's efforts towards socio-economic development and poverty alleviation by hampering governance and vitiating the investment climate. It appears inevitable that in the period up 2025 the southern Asian region and its extended neighbourhood will see a continuation of ongoing conflicts without major let up. In fact, the situation in Afghanistan and Pakistan could deteriorate beyond the ability of the international community to control it effectively.

MEETING EXTERNAL THREATS

India's major external threats emanate from the unresolved territorial disputes between India and China, and India and Pakistan. The almost unbridled scourge of radical extremism that is sweeping across the strategic landscape to India's west magnifies the intensity of the threat from Pakistan. In May 1998, India and Pakistan had crossed the nuclear Rubicon and declared themselves states armed with nuclear weapons. Tensions are inherent in the possession of nuclear weapons by neighbours with a long history of conflict. The latest manifestation of this long-drawn conflict is the almost 30-year old state-sponsored 'proxy war' waged by Pakistan's ISI-controlled mercenary terrorists against the Indian state.

While there was some nuclear sabre-rattling between India and Pakistan, particularly during the Kargil conflict, the two nations have never come close to a situation of deterrence breakdown. The "ugly stability" that is prevailing can be attributed primarily to India's unwavering strategic restraint in the face of grave provocation, democratic checks and balances in its policy processes and tight civilian control over its nuclear forces. The Pakistan army, which also controls the country's nuclear arsenal, has lost India's trust after the Kargil conflict and the terrorist strikes at Mumbai. It is capable of once again stepping up trans-LoC terrorism or even engendering a Kargil-like situation that could escalate to a major war.

India's border with China has been relatively more stable than that with Pakistan. However, China is in physical occupation of 38,000 sq km of Indian territory in Ladakh, J&K, and China claims the entire Indian state of Arunachal Pradesh (96,000 sq km) in the north-east, particularly the Tawang tract. Even the Line of Actual Control (LAC) has not been demarcated on the ground and on military maps. Recently China has exhibited unprecedented assertiveness in its diplomacy and military posture. The India-China military stand-off at Doklam in Bhutan in June-August 2017 is an example of this assertiveness. Until the territorial dispute between the two countries is resolved satisfactorily, another border conflict cannot be ruled out even though the probability is quite low.

China's increasing diplomatic, political and military assertiveness towards India at the tactical level, including multiple and frequent transgressions across the LAC, underline the existential military threat from China that is inherent in the relationship between the two countries. Also, China does not recognise India as a state armed with nuclear weapons and demands that India should go back to a non-nuclear status in terms of UNSC Resolution 1172 and, hence, refuses to discuss nuclear confidence building measures (CBMs) and nuclear risk reduction measures (NRRMs) with India.

China is engaged in the strategic encirclement of India and poses a long-term strategic challenge as a geo-political competitor and rival for markets and energy security in Asia. While the probability of conventional conflict in the near future is low, it cannot be altogether ruled out. The collusive nexus between China and Pakistan and their rapidly growing "all-weather" friendship have led most analysts in India to believe that India may have to face a two-front situation with nuclear overtones during any future conflict and must, therefore, formulate a politico-military strategy to counter it. India is moving towards the deployment of the Agni-4 and Agni-5 MRBMs and the third leg of its triad, i.e. nuclear-powered submarines armed with submarine-launched nuclear-tipped ballistic missiles (SSBN with SLBMs). This will give India genuine nuclear deterrence capability so as to prevent deterrence breakdown and reduce the risk of nuclear exchanges in any future conflict.

The threats and challenges to India's maritime security are increasing exponentially as the world turns more and more towards the exploitation of ocean resources for food, energy and raw materials. Oil platforms and drilling rigs for oil and gas exploration face a threat from marine terrorists. Increasing piracy at sea and the possible use of India's island territories by terrorist organisations and by smugglers for trade in contraband goods are other serious maritime threats. The security of India's island territories has now acquired added significance. A cohesive maritime security strategy needs to be incorporated in the management of national security so that India's ocean resources in its exclusive economic zone (EEZ) are not poached at will by state and non-state actors and Indian ships are safe and secure.

Energy and water security, as also the adverse implications of climate change and environmental pollution are among the so-called "non-traditional" threats to national security. As witnessed in the exodus of almost two million Rohingya refugees from the Rakhine province of Myanmar in 2016-17, mass migrations remain a long-term threat. Still newer challenges that are emerging include those from the proliferation of small arms, the circulation of fake currency notes, organised crime and narco-terrorism. India is flanked by two of the most notorious narcotics producing regions in the world–the Golden Crescent (Afghanistan, Iran and Pakistan; annual production approximately 2,500 tonnes) on the west and the Golden Triangle (Laos, Myanmar and Thailand; 1,500 tonnes) on the east. All of these threats and challenges need to be addressed in a coordinated, holistic, manner at the national level in conjunction with the state governments.

The prevailing security environment in southern Asia is not conducive to long-term strategic stability. India is developing robust military capabilities and is in the process of upgrading its military strategy against China from dissuasion to deterrence by raising a mountain Strike Corps with ancillary support units. However, if it is actually engaged on two fronts during a future war with China and Pakistan, at best India will be able to fight only a defensive holding action designed to deny a major breakthrough and minimise the loss of territory. Clearly, other means must be found to increase India's comprehensive national power (CNP) to deter war and ensure that India is never required to fight at least a two-front war. Military alliances are passé and India would not prefer to enter into one, but India's military power can and must be supplemented with astute diplomacy.

Strategic partnerships are one rung below military allowances and while these can lead to joint military operations when both partners are of the view that it is in their mutual interest, they do not impose any such obligation. India's major strategic partnerships should be sufficiently strong to impose caution and thereby deter aggression. Though it was not a military alliance, the Treaty of Peace, Friendship and Cooperation, which India had signed with the erstwhile Soviet Union before the 1971 war, had ensured that China refrained from aiding Pakistan militarily during the war. The Indo-US strategic partnership has been described as India's 'principal' strategic partnership. It is a hedging strategy for both against possible Chinese military adventurism. Its defence cooperation element must be taken to the next higher trajectory–intelligence sharing, joint threat assessment, joint contingency planning and the conduct of joint operations to overcome the threat when the vital national interests of both are threatened simultaneously. This will ensure that a situation similar to 1971 obtains in future and India's military adversaries are deterred from ganging up against the country.

In keeping with its growing regional responsibilities, India has been steadily enhancing its capabilities for military intervention in order to undertake out-of-area contingency operations when it becomes necessary. Though India supports UN Security Council sanction for military interventions, the country may join future coalitions of the willing even without UN approval when its vital national interests are threatened and need to be defended. It is in India's interest to encourage the establishment of a cooperative security framework for the Indo-Pacific region and work with all strategic partners and other friendly countries toward that end. The armed forces must work together to synergise joint warfare capabilities for intervention operations in India's area of strategic interest so that a rising India soon becomes a net contributor to security in the Indian Ocean region, together with strategic partners such as the United States. To achieve these goals India must raise two rapid reaction-cum-air assault divisions with the necessary aerial and ground-based firepower resources, air lift and amphibious landing capabilities by the end of the 14th Defence Plan (2022-27).

ORGANISING INTERNAL SECURITY

India's internal security environment has been vitiated by Pakistan's almost three-decade old proxy war in Jammu and Kashmir, continuing insurgency in several of India's north-eastern states, the rising tide of Maoist or Naxalite (left wing) extremism in Central India and the new wave of urban terrorism, which peaked with the dastardly attacks in Mumbai on 26 November 2008. Besides Central and State government paramilitary and police forces, the Indian Army has been deployed in large numbers to gain control over internal uprisings, some of which are supported, sponsored and militarily aided by inimical foreign powers. However, India's fightback is haphazard and lacks coherence, both in the formulation of strategy and its successful execution. The acquisition and dissemination of intelligence for preventing terrorist strikes are also patently flawed.

Though the government has moved to create NSG hubs in four metros in addition to New Delhi and has created a National Investigation Agency for post-incident investigations, clearly much more needs to be done to counter the increasing menace of urban terrorism. The UPA government did attempt to establish a National Counter-terrorism Centre (NCTC), but had been unable to forge a national consensus around the concept. As terrorism has become a major international threat, it is becoming increasingly necessary to develop counter-terrorism cooperation with India's strategic partners like the United States, including intelligence sharing, so as to fight the menace together with synergised capabilities.

A coordinated approach involving all organs of the state is necessary to formulate and implement a broad-based national-level strategy to fight internal challenges to national security. The government must draw up a comprehensive internal security strategy that is inter-ministerial, inter-agency and inter-departmental in character. Only then will various stakeholders feel empowered to take ownership of the strategy and work unitedly to achieve its aims and objectives. Such a strategy must also balance the interests of the Central and the State governments. Also, the internal security function of the Ministry of Home Affairs (MHA) should be hived off into a separate ministry headed by a cabinet minister as it requires full-time ministerial attention.

EFFORTS TOWARDS CONFLICT RESOLUTION

The ultimate aim of a nation's armed forces is to deter war; fighting and winning become necessary only if deterrence breaks down. As the primary underlying cause of future conventional conflict on the Indian sub-continent is likely to be unresolved territorial and boundary disputes, it is necessary to speedily resolve the existing disputes. Despite almost 20 rounds of talks between India's National Security Advisor and China's Vice Foreign Minister, the designated interlocutors, it has not been possible to make major headway in the resolution of the India-China territorial dispute. In fact, it has not even been possible to demarcate the Line of Actual Control on the ground and on military maps so as to prevent frequent complaints about intrusions and transgressions and to minimise the probability of an armed clash between patrols. China's intransigence and its recent claims to Tawang have led to a stalemate in negotiations. On its part India must continue to impress on the Chinese leadership the importance of the early resolution of the territorial and boundary dispute. Simultaneously, India must continue its efforts to improve border infrastructure and create adequate offensive operations capability to deter another round of conflict.

Resolution of the dispute with Pakistan over Jammu and Kashmir is equally complex as, besides India and Pakistan, the people of J&K—straddling the Line of Control (LoC)—are also a party to the conflict. While some progress had been made during the Manmohan Singh-Musharraf years, the General's troubles at home led him to back off. A ray of hope had emerged once again with the installation of an elected civilian government in Pakistan but the terror strikes in Mumbai in November 2008 brought the rapprochement process to a halt. Neither government has made any effort to mould public opinion for a possible solution. Entrenched political and religious constituencies on both the sides are likely to noisily stall any understanding that the two governments might reach. Unless the deep state in Pakistan changes its strategy of bleeding India through a thousand cuts, it is difficult to be optimistic about the early resolution of the Kashmir dispute.

In stark contrast with the difficulties of conflict resolution on the external front, there has been a fair amount of progress in resolving internal conflicts during the last ten years. The central government's cease-fire with the Nagas, which had held fairly well for over a decade even while internecine quarrels among the Nagas had continued unabated, had led to tangible progress in negotiations with both the Issak-Muivah and the Khaplang factions of the NSCN and there was cause for optimism about the early resolution of the long-drawn conflict. However, the Khaplang faction has now opted out, leading to a slowdown in the tempo for reaching a negotiated settlement. The ULFA in Assam has begun negotiations with the central government without any pre-conditions except for the break-away military wing led by Paresh Barua who is said to be taking shelter in Myanmar and is getting covert support from the Chinese. It is to be hoped that the ULFA leadership will act in a statesman-like manner for the good of the people of Assam rather than continue to pursue power for its own sake.

There is less cause for optimism regarding resolution of the conflict being waged by Maoist or Naxalite insurgents in almost 220 districts of Central India. The leadership of the CPI (Maoist) seeks to one day fly its flag from the ramparts of the Red Fort in Delhi and is pursuing its aim methodically and systematically. Despite the central government's offer for talks, it continues to indulge in wanton acts of violence, kidnappings and extortion. A comprehensive three-pronged strategy that simultaneously emphasises security, development and governance–with skilful perception management interwoven into it—is necessary to defeat the menace of left Wing Extremism (LWE). The government must also invest in the modernisation of the central and state government police forces and improve their training standards.

MANAGING NATIONAL SECURITY

There is an urgent requirement to formulate a comprehensive National Security Strategy (NSS), including internal security. The NSS should be formulated after carrying out an inter-departmental, inter-agency, multi-disciplinary strategic defence review. At present, defence procurement is being undertaken through ad hoc annual procurement plans, rather than being based on duly prioritised long-term plans that are designed to systematically enhance India's combat potential. The government must commit itself to supporting long-term defence plans or else defence modernisation will continue to lag and the growing military capabilities gap with China's People's Liberation Army will assume ominous proportions. This can be done only by reviving the dormant National Security Council as defence planning is in the domain of the NSC and not the Cabinet Committee on Security (CCS), which deals with current and near term threats and challenges and reacts to emergent situations.

Today, the concept of national security encompasses many more facets of security and is much more wide ranging than merely the defence of territory. While there is a Defence Minister of Cabinet rank, the other aspects of national security are the responsibility of the NSA. However, the NSA is only an advisor to the Prime Minister and has no executive authority. He is also not answerable to Parliament. It is necessary to upgrade the post of NSA to that of a Minister of State (MoS). He could be a MoS in the PMO and should be directly answerable to the PM. The NSA should be the chief coordinator between the three key ministries responsible for national security: MoD, MEA and MHA. He should be given executive control over the external and internal intelligence agencies. He should also be nominated as India's cyber Tsar and given the responsibility to coordinate cyber security as well as offensive cyber operations.

The government must also immediately appoint a Chief of Defence Staff (CDS) or a permanent Chairman of the Chiefs of Staff Committee to provide single-point advice to the CCS on military matters. Any further dithering on this key structural reform in higher defence management on the grounds of the lack of political consensus and the inability of the armed forces to agree on the issue will be extremely detrimental to India's interests in the light of the dangerous developments taking place in India's neighbourhood. The logical next step would be to constitute tri-Service integrated theatre commands to synergise the capabilities of individual Services. International experience shows that such reform has to be imposed form the top down and can never work if the government keeps waiting for it to come about from the bottom up.

While internal security challenges are gradually gaining prominence, preparations for conventional conflict must not be neglected. Major defence procurement decisions must be made quickly. Large-scale ammunition shortages have been pointed out in several Comptroller and Auditor General (CAG) reports in 2015-17. These must be made up quickly. Many tanks and infantry combat vehicles are still 'night blind'—they lack suitable night vision equipment. The army is still without towed and self-propelled 155mm howitzers for the plains and urgently needs new utility helicopters, anti-tank guided missiles (ATGMs) as also to acquire weapons and equipment for counter-insurgency operations. The navy waited for long for the Vikramaditya (Admiral Gorshkov) aircraft carrier, which was being refurbished in a Russian shipyard at exorbitant cost and with operationally crippling time overruns. Construction of the indigenous air defence ship and Scorpene submarines is behind schedule.

The plans of the air force to acquire 126 multi-mission, medium-range combat aircraft (MMRCA) in order to maintain its edge over the regional air forces is stuck in the procurement quagmire except that a contract has been signed for the acquisition of 36 Rafale fighter aircraft. The LCA project continues to lag way behind schedule. Meanwhile, the MiG-21 and MiG-27 fleets have become obsolescent. The IAF needs more AWACS aircraft and air-to-air refuellers, besides additional transport aircraft. All three Services need a large number of light and medium lift helicopters. India's nuclear forces require the Agni-4 and Agni-5 missiles and nuclear-powered submarines with suitable ballistic missiles to acquire genuine deterrent capability against China. The armed forces do not have a truly integrated C4I2SR system for network-centric warfare, which will allow them to optimise their individual capabilities and enable the conduct of effects-based operations. Force multipliers like combat drones (UCAVs) are yet to be introduced into service.

All of these high-priority acquisitions will require extensive budgetary support. With the defence budget languishing at less than 1.6 per cent of India's GDP at present—compared with China's 3.5 per cent and Pakistan's 4.5 per cent—it will not be possible for the armed forces to undertake any meaningful modernisation or make up equipment and ammunition deficiencies. The funds available on the capital account at present are inadequate to suffice even for the replacement of obsolete weapons systems and obsolescent equipment that are still in service well beyond their useful life cycles. The central armed police forces (CAPFs) also need to be modernised as they are facing qualitatively greater threats while continuing to be equipped with sub-standard weapons. The defence budget must be substantially enhanced to enable the armed forces to meet future threats and challenges, as also to discharge India's obligations and fulfil the country's responsibilities towards making a positive contribution to peace and stability in the Indo-Pacific region. Only then will the environment be conducive to rapid socio-economic development.

Brig Gurmeet Kanwal (Retd)
Distinguished Fellow,
Institute for Defence Studies and Analyses,
New Delhi and former Director,
Centre for Land Warfare Studies (CLAWS), New Delhi.

XII

Sabka Saath, Sabka Vikas! Chalein, Saath Saath!

– Surendra Kumar

No rational person, irrespective of the language he speaks, the faith he follows, the political ideology he believes in and the nation he hails from, can possibly have any objections to this noble thought. It has universal appeal transcending national boundaries. Its truism is timeless; it could be used by any ruler anywhere at any time, from Emperor Ashok to Emperor to Emperor Akbar and from Jawaharlal Nehru to Narendra Damodar Modi! No wonder John Kerry, the US Secretary of State, called it a "great vision" on his official visit to India in Aug 2014.

This is so all embracing; it can be adopted by the UN as one of its major goals! Without sincere and serious pursuit of this vision, it's impossible to achieve SDGs of the UN. In its underlying humanistic message, inspiring objective and the intrinsic values it espouses, this idea is as lofty as the concept of Vasudhiava Kutumbkam! If it is implemented in letter and spirit, it can transform India. PM Modi deserves to be applauded, by his friends and foes alike, for putting forward this idea.

In nut shell, it encapsulates the philosophy of the Preamble of India's Constitution. It could be a guiding compass for good governance and addressing pressing domestic issues. If pursued with prudence, pragmatism and sensitivity, it can be equally effective and productive in conducting external relations, bilateral, regional and international. But while, at public rallies and TV debates, it may be a sound argument to win brownie points; this seemingly simple Mantra is hard to implement.

Inclusiveness is the essence of this concept; Sabka Saath presupposes taking along everybody. It implies non-discrimination of all kinds and in all forms. The State becomes the upholder and the guarantor of equality, non-discrimination and inclusiveness. When none can be left behind or denied his/her due because of the religion, the State has no option but to be secular; letting the followers of all faiths pursue and practice their respective faiths; none is allowed to intimidate others and claim superiority of one's faith over others.'

It also means, people should be able to get along with their lives following their customs, beliefs, food habits, dresses and numerous cultural manifestations of their creativity without being told to abide by certain diktas. It means the celebration of India's bewildering diversity and letting thousands flowers of ideas bloom presenting a riot of colours and spreading uplifting fragrances all around.

Sabka Vikas implores the govt of the day not only to be non-discriminatory in the pursuit of growth and progress but to proactively strive for development of all. As all don't set out at the same stage, for ensuring Sabka Vikas, even at the risk of being called Leftist/Socialist/ Communist, the govt has to introduce special schemes/ initiatives to meet special needs of those who have been disadvantaged for centuries. It becomes the principal enabler and capacity and capability builder of those sections of society. In a country like India where people live at different level of development simultaneously, affirmative action and positive discrimination, solely driven by national developmental agenda, not by electoral calculations and considerations, becomes unavoidable. Such measures need to be assessed and evaluated periodically for judging their efficacy and resetting them to produce expected positive change in the conditions of the targeted sections of the society.

Chalein Saath Saath takes for granted high standards of tolerance, understanding and appreciation of each other. You don't enjoy walking with anyone with whom you can't have a decent conversation which will invariably imply discussion, exchange of ideas and tolerance of different and, at times, contrarian point of view. Who wants to walk with someone who expects you to nod your head in supplication; who doesn't allow you to have your say, who underlines his authority and insists on "my way or high way"?

It also implies, you are cognizant of and sensitive to other's pain and anguish and believe in caring and sharing. Gandhi's favourite bhajan: vaishnav jan te, tene kahiye, pir parayi jane re ... sums up the social responsibility of the Govt and the society at large. Alas, in India, the spirit of caring and sharing in most of the cases is confined to pious words rather than in commensurate actions.

In spite of his humble upbringing Narendra Modi has evolved into an effective administrator and one of the shrewdest politicians of India. He thinks big, acts big and unfolds a grand vision for India; he has announced more policies and schemes which directly and indirectly affect our lives than any other Prime Minister since independence. A 24x7 Presidential PM, he seems to harbour the notion that he is destined to transform India as never before. The taste of pudding is in eating and the test of policies is in their implementation. If even 65% of what he has promised gets implemented and produces desired results, he will go down in India's history as the most transformative PM of India. If not, he will be accused of being a dream merchant who shows enchanting dreams but they largely remain dreams; there is supposedly a huge gulf between what he promises and what he actually delivers on the ground. High sounding promises, mesmerising oratory and mastery on rhetoric, if unaccompanied by corresponding concrete results, seldom bring about far reaching and long term changes.

Barring a pre-emptive strike against Iran by Israel, ostensibly to halt Iran's alleged pursuit of acquiring nuclear weapons, with tacit or overt support from the US, and Iran's retaliatory action against the Gulf States which may plunge the entire region in to an unprecedented chaos inflicting inescapable collateral damage on large oil importing countries, India's GDP should grow at an annual rate of 7-8 % till 2022, if not higher. But it shouldn't be taken as given. Even without an open hostility between Israel-US and Iran, the continuing escalation in the price of crude oil and steep slide in the value of Indian currency will have a cascading effect on India's economy impacting negatively many plans and schemes of the Govt with political and social ramifications.

While rising to 100 place from 142 place on the scale of Ease of Doing Business is laudable, it also underlines what a long journey lies ahead to join the group of first 20.Whichever Govt is at the helm of affairs at the Centre, must continue improving Ease of Doing Business in India and keep the economy open, adaptable and competitive in spite of the protectionist policies followed by the US and it's trade war with China which entails negative repercussions for the entire world.

Evidently, having good relations with the US is a Must for access to cutting edge, higher and innovative technologies and for meeting long inventories of the three wings of our Defence Force for the latest defence equipments and hedging against China's regional and global ambitions. Nonetheless, we shouldn't slide into America's embrace too tight for comfort and lose our autonomy of strategic decision making. Though 30+ bilateral dialogues mechanisms covering a wide range of areas and joint military exercises are beneficial to India and the US and India have convergence of visions for Indo-pacific region, we can't allow the PM of India representing 1.35 billion people publicly mocked and mimicked by a billionaire turned President of the US . By signing LEMOA and COMCASA we have overcome the hesitation of history as has the US by assigning STA-1 status to India for transfer of sensitive technologies. We must draw certain red lines for conduct of our bilateral relations and leverage billions of dollars worth defence deals we are signing with the US. If the US really considers India as her strategic partner and major Defence partner, it should be sensitive to India's national needs and not expect abject surrender to its highly objectionable extraterritorial application of CAATSA and welcome sanctions for doing business with Iran and Russia. SA-400 is essential for our national security; the Modi govt took the right decision to sign the agreement during the visit of the Russian President Putin (5-6 October 2018) taking a calculated risk of imposition of the US sanctions. Similarly, Iranian oil contributes to India's energy security. It's high time, we explain, to the US firmly our terms of friendship. Where hugs fail plain speaking might succeed. As America First is the anthem for Trump, India First is the Mantra for Modi. For a lasting friendship, Twin should meet.

Thanks to the unconventional, unorthodox, undiplomatic, disruptive and transactional approach of the present US President to foreign relations and threats to exit from International agreements when he can't have his way, International relations are likely to remain in a flux. His bullying style and preference to conduct foreign relations through tweets on bilateral, regional and global issues makes matters worse. If he gets a second terms, not unlikely, international scenario won't change much by 2022. Retaining her relations with countries with which Trump is having a running battle of words which can degenerate into open conflicts, India will have to remain alert, agile and flexible not to get caught in the cross fire and protect her national interests.

American relations with China, Russia and Iran are bound to impact India. However, increasing Sino-American tension also motivates both to woo India as never before. Should we be complaining? Crippling US sanctions are pushing Russia closer to China; history of recent past tells us that a closer Russian-Chinese axis hasn't served India's long term interests. With more than 70% of our Defence requirements still met by Russia, defence trade remains the strongest glue for Indo-Russian relations; bilateral trade is still modest; at the Modi-Putin Summit in Delhi in October 2018 the mention of a target of US$ 30 billion in the next five years underlines this reality.

While Trump has already taken the US out of COP-21 Paris Climate Change Agreement, Modi's initiative on International Solar Alliance and greater use of alternative and renewable sources of energy has earned him international praise. The "Champion of Earth" Award for 2018, the highest UN environmental award, was bestowed upon him along with the French President Emmanuel Macron, by the UN Secretary General Antonio Guterres in Delhi on 3 October 2018. The citation read, "UN Environment is recognising Indian Prime Minister Narendra Modi for his bold environmental leadership on the global stage. Under Modi's leadership, India pledged to eliminate all single-use plastics in the country by 2022. Prime Minister Modi also supports and champions the International Solar Alliance, a global partnership to scale up solar energy."

The Indian govt must continue to push its environment friendly policies vigorously. Every winter, Delhi is covered with thick cloud of smog; burning of crop stubbles in Haryana and Punjab is a factor. The Govt must show political will and muscles to ban stubble burning and take stern actions against the violators of infrastructural and industrial pollution control measures; it shouldn't wait for the Courts to intervene.

Donald Trump will land a serious blow to free and fair international trading system if he walks out of the WTO. The US Congress and like-minded nations, both developing and developed, should pressure him against such a negative step. Irrespective of his move, the votaries of free trade should strengthen bilateral as well as regional agreements to expand and deepen free and rule based international trade.

The fissures in the US-European alliance, unless checked and repaired soon, will have serious global repercussions. Nonetheless, it might also open new opportunities for India as the European countries would be looking for alternative markets and investment opportunities.

Modi's outreach to Africa has been unprecedented. Besides holding India-Africa summit in Delhi in October 2015, more visits to Africa by the President/Vice President and PM have taken place in the last four years than in the last 40 years! This enhanced interaction develops deeper trust and confidence which should result in greater collaborative and mutually productive convergence, especially as several African countries are becoming wary of China's aggressive forays leading to long term debt trap. There is every reason to believe that India and Africa will come still closer by 2022.

While we work together with leading Latin American Countries like Brazil, Argentina and Mexico in International Forums like the UN and the G-20 and India's economic relations with them and other countries like Cuba, Venezuela, Bolivia, Paraguay and Uruguay have expanded, India's over all trade with and investment in South America lags far behind China. India ought to expand and enhance her outreach with this region; it will have mutually beneficial economic and strategic outcome.

Though Narsimha Rao and Manmohan Singh pursued Look East" policy towards ASEAN and South East Asian countries, Modi is doing it much more vigorously. He hasn't merely changed the nomenclature calling it "Act East policy" but enhanced exponentially the level of exchanges and interaction with them .If the 21st century is going to be the Century of Asia, it won't happen only on account of China, Japan and India but, to a great extent, also because of the economic vibrancy of the ASEAN and South East countries. Modi's mantra of 3 Cs: Connectivity, Commerce and Culture offers the right mix of historical and cultural links with today's requirements of connectivity, trade and business and investment. China's increasing assertiveness in South China Sea and territorial claims against several countries of the region seem to have made them more amenable to expansion of their ties with India .China is the largest trading partner for most of them so, they can't afford to antagonise her. But in their calculation, closer and warmer relations with India can somewhat hedge them against China's pressure.

In uncertain and turbulent times when Trump threatens to impose tariffs on any country that doesn't fall in line with his notion of what's right, India is smartly deepening and expanding its economic integration with Asian countries as evident from her renewed thrust to make BIMSTEC and RCEP work. A clear realization that progress of these organizations will also lead to economic development of India's North East region is a motivating factor. India won't like to project the QUAD as an anti China Group but it isn't averse to its revival, at least, at a lower level. With this backdrop, it was a brilliant idea on the part of PM Modi to invite all the Heads of State of the ASEAN countries as the Chief Guests at the Republic Day parade on 26 January 2018. India and the ASEAN and South East Asian countries are likely to come still closer by 2022.

Modi'd endeavours to draw the gulf countries, particularly Saudi Arabia and UAE, closer to India and distance them from Pakistan, at least, with regard to fighting terrorism, are bearing some fruits. This outreach must expand to other Gulf countries without supporting Saudi Arbia against Iran.

All nations are, expectedly, safeguarding their national interests in the face of strategic churning in the Indo-Pacific region brought to the fore by policies of the Donald Trump and Xi Jinping, the ambitious "Core Leader" in China. In this state of flux, Modi's "Sabka Saath and Sabka Vikas" can prove to be a sensible and sensitive way of conducting external relations with the countries of this region.

Modi started his inning as the PM with the laudable: "Neighbours First" approach and took several initiatives to generate warmth in India's relations with her immediate neighbours. His invitation to the Heads of States of all the SAARC nations and Afghanistan was an example of Out Of Box and innovative diplomacy. He has under taken more bilateral visits to neighbouring countries than most of his predecessors; unfortunately, the results have been a mixed bag. With the hind sight, it appears, his unprecedented gesture like dropping by Nawaz Sharif's home in Lahore on his birthday on 25 December 2015 as well as strong action like surgical strike against launch pads across the LOC (30 September 2016) haven't produced the desired results; neither Pakistan has stopped terrorist attacks on India from its soil nor dismantled Terrorists infrastructure and training camps nor stopped infiltration in Jammu and Kashmir. Blowing hot and cold about holding talks with Pakistan hasn't earned us any leverage either; it has instead given Pakistan a publicity pretext to project India as intransigent neighbour disinterested in peace and tranquillity in South Asia. The relationship with Pakistan isn't likely to change drastically by 2022 as the Army and the ISI continue to call the shots so far as the defence and foreign policy towards India and Afghanistan is concerned irrespective whether the elected Civilian Govt is headed by Nawaz Sharif or Imran Khan. Dastardly attack on the CRPF convoy at Pulwama causing more than 40 deaths proves that. India's pre-emptive non-military air strike at JeM's training camps in Balakot in Pakistan's Khyber Pakhtunwa region in early hours on 26 February 2019 which is believed to have eliminated many trainers, commanders and terrorists including Yousuf Azhar, brother in law of Masood Azhar, will hopefully have a sobering effect on terrorists operating from Pakistan and from the region.

Attempts by 22 Pakistani fighter planes which included 10 F-16 to drop bombs across the LoC in India, early morning on 27 February, were foiled when they were challenged by Indian air force fighters. In the ensuing dog fight, one F-16 of Pakistan was shot by India and an Indian MIG 21 was downed by Pakistan. It also resulted in the capture of Indian Pilot Abhinandan Varthaman who had fallen inside Pakistan. While the charged up situation has de-escalated after the release of Abhinandan under international pressure and his return to India, we haven't heard the last word on India-Pakistan tension.

Bhutan was the first country Modi visited after becoming Prime Minister; India's relations with this scenic, mountainous country remain close in spite of 73 days long military standoff between India and China on Dhoklam plateau in Bhutan (disengagement began on 26 Aug 2017) and China's pressure on Bhutan. However, India must remain vigilant as Dhoklam like test of India's resolve and defence preparedness by China shouldn't be ruled out in coming years.

Modi's first visit to the only Hindu nation on earth, Nepal had left a positive impact. But subsequent agitation by Madhesh is and people from Terai against the newly drafted constitution which short shifted their legitimate rights and blockade of supply trucks for 3 months suggest that the handlers of India's relations with Nepal took eyes off the ball and let things drift. By reaching out to K.P. Sharma Oli and Ramchandra Dahal and dangling economic goodies, India's struggling to retain her traditional influence in Nepal's polity which is being eroded fast by China's infrastructural and financial inroads. By finalising the Protocol (7 September 2018) of a Transit and Transport Agreement (TRA 2016) which now offers 7 Chinese transit points: four sea ports (Tianjin (Xingang), Shenzhen, Lianyungang, Zhanjiang) and three land ports (Lanzhou, Lhasa, Xigatse)—to Nepal for trade with third countries, China is breaching Nepal's long dependence on India for trade and external connectivity. Nepal is reportedly urging China to extend its railway line from Tibet to Kathmandu; China is lukewarm as running this railway facility might not be economically viable. To ally India's apprehensions China's Foreign Minister Wang Yi said during Nepali FM P. K. Gyawali's visit in September 2018 that China was willing to extend this corridor to India thus Nepal could benefit from both India China. India sees this yet another Chinese attempt at getting India on board for BRI. By pledging to build US$ 2.5 billion worth 1200 megawatt Hydal power plant on Budhi Gandaki, the largest in Nepal, China is trying to wean Nepal away from India's special relationship. In coming years, India will have to compete and contend with China in Nepal whose leaders, irrespective of their political affiliations, will like to play China card against India.

China is not a member of the SAARC; not yet, though Pakistan has been advocating for its inclusion. But its influence in South Asia has grown substantially in recent years; except India and Bhutan all countries have embraced Xi Jinping's gigantic pet project BRI willing or hesitatingly. The handing over of 85% shares of Hambantota port built by China during pro China President Mahinda Rajapaksha's tenure for 99 years for US$1.2 billion in Dec 2017 is turning in to a debt trap for Sri Lanka. Though China has assured that the port to be run by two Chinese companies: Hambantota International Port Group (HIPG) and Hambantota International Port Services (HIPS) and the Sri Lanka Ports Authority, will not be used for military purposes one will have to take these assurances with a pinch of salt. After all, Rajapakshs did allow a PLAN Song class Chinese submarine to visit this port; the use of Hambantota by the PLA in emergency situation can't be ruled out. This port on the southern coast of Sri Lanka offers China a strategic opening on the Indian Ocean. Obviously, India can't match China's freebies in Sri Lanka, growing wariness about China's debt trap and deft and sensitive diplomacy can still retain India's special relationship built over decades and strengthened by geographical, historical, cultural, religious and ethnic links between the two countries.

Maldives, the tiny archipelago in Indian Ocean, a member of SAARC, has been causing concern to India with its growing closeness to China under President Abdullah Yameen who has not only joined the BRI but also signed several financing and investment deals with

China with total disregard to India's sensitivity. As 80% of its debt is owed to China alone, a debt trap similar to that of Sri Lanka looms large. India can't give a blind eye to China's growing inroads in Maldives which has allowed Chinese submarines to visit its port. Maldives sits astride on the sea lanes through which pass most of Indian cargo ships and Indian's naval station on Lakshadweep Island of Minicoy is just 100 KM; Indian strategic concerns are understandable.

Increasing Saudi influence and deepening of Wahabi radicalisation in Maldives (many Maldivians have gone to fight for ISIS in Syria and Iraq) pose threat of terrorist attacks on India. In 2016 Yameen govt cancelled the contract of US$ 511 million awarded to GMR on questionable grounds and awarded a contract of US$ 800 to Saudi Arabia's Binladen group underlining Saudi clout. To safeguard her backwater, India will have to adopt an imaginative and proactive approach in her relations with Maldives. Ibrahim Mohamed Solih's election as the next President offers a welcome opportunity for India to recalibrate relationship with Maldives.

During Modi's Premiership, India's relations with Bangladesh have been on the mend and witnessed a degree of trust and confidence in spite of massive Chinese investment in Bangladesh and political rhetoric in India about the repatriation of immigrants from Bangladesh and refugees from Myanmar. The Land boundary Agreement, signed by Indira Gandhi and Muzibur Rehman in1974, eventually got implemented following Modi-Hasina agreement(June 2015) to swap selected enclaves on the border. Sheikh Hasina has handed over several Insurgents leaders wanted in India; she has also honoured many Indian Civilian and Military personalities who had played a crucial role in the birth of Bangladesh and is sensitive in addressing India's concerns about threat of terrorism. Radicalisation of Bangladeshi youth is on the rise thanks to terrorist groups in Pakistan and inflow of funds from Saudi Arabia. Cooperation in counter terrorism endeavours between India and Bangladesh helps both the countries and ought to be augmented.

Connectivity is the buzz word for the success of India's "Act East policy"and economic development of North Eastern states. Road and rail connectivity between India and Bangladesh not only facilitates movement of people but drastically cuts the travel time and costs of transportation of goods. The bus service between Kolkota to Agartala via Dhaka covering a distance of 910 KM operationalised on 7 June 2015 and Bandhan Express between Kolkota and Khulna (172 KM) flagged of by Modi and Hasina through video conferencing on 7 November 2017 have generated positivity, goodwill and economic activity on both sides; Maitree Express between Dhaka and Kolkota has been quite popular.

BBIN, motor vehicle agreement signed by Bangladesh, Bhutan, Nepal and India is an example of sub-regional connectivity which would regulate and facilitate vehicular movement among the signatories.

While Hasina welcomed India's decision to supply electricity to Bangldesh, her dream of signing an agreement on sharing of Teesta reviver water remains unfulfilled notwithstanding efforts of two Indian PMs: Manmohan Singh and Narendra Modi; the West Bengal, CM Mamta Banerjee continues to oppose for fear of backlash from her voters.

The issue of Bangladeshi immigrants who have been living in India for long has political sensitivity at election time as many of them traditionally support certain parties. Besides, involvement of some of the radicalised youth among them in terrorist attacks in J&K has introduced considerable negativity about them. According to the draft NRC, over 4 million of such immigrants having lived in Assam for decades aren't legally Indians citizens creating a huge political row in India. Arrival of Rohingyas from Myanmar through Bangladesh and the question of their repatriation have added further complications; some Indian political parties, foreign Govt.'s and the UN have expressed concern. These issues should be handled with understanding, humanitarian needs, prevailing realities on the ground and practical and feasible measures.

By 2022, India's relations with her neighbours will demand mature and pragmatic handling. Internal political and economic developments in each of them and deep inroads which China has made will have to be born in mind while pursuing our national interest. While "Gujral Doctrine" is viewed with disdain in the corridors of power and by diplomatic and political Pandits in India, a strategy which embraces the spirit of Gujral doctrine might serve our interests and counter China's increasing influence in South Asia. The days of the Big Brother expecting automatic acknowledgement and accommodation of our wishes and sensitivities are passé. Instead, India will have to win over her neighbours with multi-pronged approach underlining our magnanimity, willingness to help without hoping for equal reciprocity and use of tact and quiet diplomacy away from the combustible political rhetoric. Isn't this the true spirit of Sabka Saath, Sabka Vikas?

India's border dispute with China still remains unresolved. Chinese Incursions into Indian Territory do take place often though there has been no open hostility at the border for decades. During President Xi Jinping's visit in September 2014, 1000 PLA soldiers had crossed over in to Chumar sector of Ladhak and stayed put for weeks though the issue was raised with Xi himself. Military standoff between China and India occurred when in June 2017 China tried to extend a road Southward from Yadong on Dhoklam plateau (in Bhutan) near Dhoklam pass which continued till 28 August 2017. China has foiled India's efforts to join the NSG; it has also stalled UN efforts to include Masood Azhar, Pakistan based leader of Jaish-e-Mohammed, UN designated Terrorist group, in the UN list of terrorists. Xi Jinping, the strongest Chinese Leader after Deng Xiaoping, is focussed on realising his Vision 2025 and matching if not overtaking the US, in cutting edge technologies, innovations and AI. Thanks to the size of her economy and military and financial resources, roughly four times larger than India and global clout and influence she has built, China isn't prepared to accept India as her equal. Nonetheless, as prominent Asian giants, India and China cooperate with each other in the BRICS, SCO, G 20, Development Bank, AIIB and Climate Change negotiations. Both Xi Jinping and Modi have emerged as the powerful voices in favour of globalisation at a time when the Donald Trump is resorting to imposition of tariffs and sanctions and damaging the WTO, Regulator of the rule based

International Trading system. Presently, there is some convergence between India and China on undertaking selected projects in Afghanistan jointly including the training of their diplomats.

India can't be oblivious of China's territorial claims against her neighbours and her assertiveness in South Sea which impact her as well. In the prevailing scenario, we have no option but to maintain peace and tranquillity on the border and deepen trust and confidence between the top leaders through Wuhan type summits and peg our China policy on three pillars: engagement, cooperation and competition. China respects power as do others. Avoiding open hostility, India must concentrate on enhancing her economic and military might and improve her relations with her immediate neighbours and the countries of ASEAN and South East Asia. Our success on these fronts will elicit a much more respectful acknowledgement from China.

Long term future of Afghanistan looks uncertain. Trump had reversed Obama's decision to exit fully by 2016 and his own campaign stance. Both Russia and China are showing greater interest in Afghanistan .President Ashraf Ghani has often accused Pakistan of supporting Terrorist groups like Haqqani that mount attacks in Afghanistan. The Taliban have also been resorting to violence to demonstrate their indispensability for a political solution. The US view that there are Good Talibans who should be brought onboard for a political solution and the Bad ones who should be dealt with a heavy hand didn't resonate with India; for her, all Taliban are terrorists who pose threat to the Civilian Govt in Afghanistan and commit terrorist attacks against India. Trump's sudden decision to withdrawn half of its troops from Afghanistan and concede to several demands of Taliban and hold talks with them with Pakistan's help will have serious repercussions for India.

India's investment of over US$ 3 billion in Afghanistan in creating infrastructure: roads, hospitals, schools, training facilities, capacity building has generated goodwill towards her. She has also conducted training courses for Afghan security personnel in India but assiduously refused to send her troops and join the ISAF. However,

Pakistan resents India's presence and accuses her Consulates, without any evidence, of using RAW agents and facilitating attacks against Pakistan. Interests of the US, Russia, China, India and Pakistan don't converge in Afghanistan; each is trying to protect its own interests; this won't change soon. India should continue taking part in the Heart of Asia conferences and stand resolutely for Afghanistan's sovereignty, territorial integrity and political stability without interference from outside.

India has become the 5 largest economy in the world and is tipped to rise to the 3 rank in the next 3 decades. Progress has never been a straight line for any nation so internal and external factors which could trip us shouldn't be ruled out. In fact, internal pitfalls pose higher danger. With 5000 year old culture, bewildering diversity, unbelievable philosophical depth, a huge reservoir of talent, exceptional ability to embrace new ideas and master new technologies, India in the 21 century should feel confident to encourage discussion, debate, expression of dissenting, even contrarian views and maturity and wisdom to argue with the argumentative Indian to arrive at a rational and well informed policy decisions which will serve larger interests of the nation. For her future progress, social cohesion, harmony, inclusiveness and a spirit of caring and sharing is a must. No individual or group or ideology can be allowed to usurp to it self the right to decide for others what is right and what's wrong or take law into one's hand, intimidate others and demand obeisance. Millions have reportedly been brought above the poverty line but millions still live in abject poverty eking out a living .Gandhi's dream of wiping tears off the cheeks of the last man in the queue is still a dream. There aren't many "vaishnav jan" in India who really understand "parai pir" and try to alleviate it. The gulf between words and actions has widened not narrowed. Might is right, my way or high way, one size fits all, success by hook or crook, insatiable greed, absence of national discipline and civic duties and utter callousness run counter to the essence of Sabka Saath, Sabka Vikas, Chalein Saath!

The Challenge for India is to transform this fascinating concept in to ground reality. The Govt. can't do it alone. Millions of brave hearts will have to work selflessly and tirelessly to make it happen.

The Contributors

SURESH PRABHAKAR PRABHU

Suresh Prabhakar Prabhu is the current Minister of Commerce and Industry of India, in the cabinet of PM Narendra Modi. He is a Chartered Accountant by profession. Since 1996, Prabhu has been a elected Member of Parliament repeatedly from Rajapur Lok Sabha constituency in Maharashtra as a member of the Shiv Sena (SS). He quit Shiv Sena and joined BJP on 9 November 2014. He currently represents Andhra Pradesh in Upper House of Indian Parliament.

Prabhu obtained his Bachelor degree in Commerce with Honours from M.L. Dahanukar College, Vile Parle, Mumbai a Bachelor's degree in Law from the New Law College (Ruparel College campus), Mumbai.

Prabhu, during the Premiership of Atal Bihari Vajpayee of 1998 to 2004, served as the Industry Minister, Minister of Environment and Forests, Minister of Fertilizers and Chemicals, Power, Heavy Industry and Public Enterprises. As the Minister of Power, he introduced major reforms in India's power sector. He is credited with championing and enacting The Electricity Act, 2003 and the reforms that created securitization of dues from the states. He has been elected to the Lok Sabha, India's parliament four terms, from Maharashtra since 1996.

Prabhu was also Chairman of Task Force for Interlinking of Rivers with a status and rank of Union Cabinet Minister. He was elected a member of the World Bank parliamentary network and chaired the South Asia Water regional group of the World Bank.

Prabhu was the Union Railway Minister of India from November 2014 to September 2017.

HARDEEP SINGH PURI

Hardeep Singh Puri, Hon'ble Minister of State **(Independent Charge)** in the Ministry of Housing and Urban Affairs. He did his BA (Hons) History from Hindu College, University of Delhi and completed his MA (History) 1973.

He joined the Indian Foreign Service in 1974. During a career spanning 39 years, served in senior positions at the Ministries of External Affairs and Defence, held ambassadorial level posts in the United Kingdom, Brazil and served as Permanent Representative of India to the United Nations both in Geneva and New York.

Hardeep Singh Puri has extensive experience in multilateral diplomacy. He served on three occasions as a member of India's delegation to the GATT/United Nations in Geneva including as Ambassador and Permanent Representative from 2002 to 2005.

He was President of the United Nations Security Council in August 2011 and November 2012 and Chairman of the United Nations Security Council Counter-Terrorism Committee in 2011-2012.

He retired from the Indian Foreign Service on 28 February 2013 and joined the International Peace Institute (IPI), New York. He was Senior Adviser from June to December 2013. He was Vice-President of the IPI and Secretary General of the Independent Commission on Multilateralism (ICM). He left the IPI on 31 March 2016.

He has authored *'Perilous Interventions'—The Security Council and the Politics of Chaos*, *India's Trade Policy Dilemma and the Role of Domestic Reform*, and Delusional Politics.

He has served as the Chairman of the Governing Council of the Research and Information Systems for Developing Countries (RIS) and is a visiting faculty of the Graduate Institute in Geneva.

He was inducted in the Union Cabinet on 3 September, 2017 and took over as Minister of State (Independent Charge) of the Ministry of Housing and Urban Affairs on 4 September 2017.

B.P. SINGH

Former Home Secretary and Former Governor

Balmiki Prasad Singh is a distinguished scholar, thinker and public servant. B. P. Singh is former Governor of Sikkim. B. P. Singh was born on 1 January 1942 in Bihar. He was educated in a village school and subsequently at the Universities of Patna and Oxford. He became lecturer in the post graduate department of Political Science of Patna University at the age of nineteen. B. P. Singh was appointed to the Indian Administrative Service (IAS) in 1964. He worked in Assam as well as with Government of India and also abroad. B. P. Singh was Culture Secretary and Home Secretary, Government of India and Executive Director and Ambassador at the World Bank, Washington, DC. B. P. Singh has been the recipient of several fellowships and awards. He has written six books.

B. P. Singh is well known as the author of the Bahudha approach, which outlines the path towards a harmonious world as against the clash of civilisations as outlined in his globally acclaimed book Bahudha and the post 9/11 World (OUP: 2008). His latest book is titled: *The 21st Century: Geo-politics, Democracy and Peace* (Routledge: New York London 2017). B. P. Singh is an eminent public speaker in English and Hindi and has delivered memorial lectures and speeches at national and global levels. B. P. Singh is currently working on the promotion of Peace, Science and Culture through his association with several organisations and by writings and speeches.

YOGENDRA NARAIN

Yogendra Narain is a former IAS officer of the 1965 batch of the UP cadre. He was the Chief Secretary of UP with the longest stint in the last two decades.

After retiring as Defence Secretary in the Govt. of India he was appointed as the Secretary General of Rajya Sabha by the Vice President of India. After demitting office he worked as Member Secretary of INTACH and later as Vice President of the Indian Trust for Rural Heritage and Development.

He has written several articles on Defence and the working of Parliament.

He has authored four books namely ABC of Public Relations for Civil Servants, Saga of Civil Services Born to Serve and Clouds and other Poems

He was the founder Chairman of the National Highways Authority of India and the Greater Noida Industrial Development Authority as well as the New Pension Scheme Trust

He was given the Paul Appleby Award for outstanding services to Public Administration by the Vice President of India in 2017.

At present he is the Chancellor of the H. N. Bahuguna Central University of Garhwal.

SUSHIL C. TRIPATHI

Sushil Chandra Tripathi (b.01/01/1946) Msc. (Phy-First class first), LLB, PG Dip in Development (Cantab), AIMA Dip in Management. He joined IAS in 1968 and retired from service on 31 December 2005.

He served in many positions in State Govt. of UP and the Govt. of India. In UP, he was Officer in Charge Mahakumbh 1976-77, founder CEO of NOIDA township (1978-80), Managing Director Industrial and Investment Corporation of UP (1980-85), Secretary in the departments of Rural Development, Panchayati Raj and 20 Point Programme (1985-86), Heavy Industry, Taxation and institutional Finance (1992-93) and Principal Secretary to Governor during President Rule (1995-96), Adviser Industry and Finance (1996-97) and Principal Secretary Finance (1997-2000).

In Govt. of India, he served as Joint Secretary, Banking (1986-87), Secretary BIFR (1987-88), Joint Secretary, Economic Affairs (1988-89), Minister (Economic and Commerce), Embassy of India, Tokyo (1989-92) and Addl. Secretary, Mines (2000-02) and CMD BALCO (2000-01) as well as CMD, NALCO (2001-02). He was Secretary to Govt. of India for nearly four years, two and half years in the departments of School Education and Literacy and Higher and

Technical Education and one and half year in Petroleum and Natural Gas.

After retirement, he is associated with a number of think tanks in Education, Energy, Economy and Governance.

M.L. KUMAWAT

Mahendra L. Kumawat is a former Director General, Border Security Force. (BSF)—the largest border guarding force in the world responsible for guarding one of the most sensitive borders (Indo-Pakistan).

During his long career spanning 37 years in the Indian Police Service (IPS; 1972 batch, Andhra Pradesh). Besides working as district Supdt. of Police and Range DIG , he was also Chief of the elite anti-Naxal Commando force, Greyhounds. He also served as Additional Director General, Law and Order, Andhra Pradesh.

While on central deputation he was Joint Director, CBI, Bombay, DG, Narcotics Control Bureau, Chairman, Ceasefire Monitoring Group Nagaland.

As Special Secretary, Internal Security in the Ministry of Home Affairs he was also involved in tackling the 26/11 Mumbai attack.

He is an alumnus and gold medalist of the National Defence College of India and has been awarded President of India's Police medal for distinguished service.

AJAY SHANKAR

Presently a Distinguished Fellow, TERI, he was a member of the premier Indian Administrative Service which he joined in 1973 and retired as Secretary, Department of Industrial Policy and Promotion in the Government of India in December, 2009. He played a crucial role in putting together the stimulus packages at the time of the global economic crisis of 2008 which enabled the Indian economy to recover in a short time and again grow at over 8%. The plan for the ambitious Delhi-Mumbai Industrial Corridor Project was developed under his stewardship. He was the Chairman of the National Productivity Council and of the Quality Council of India. He served for a three year term, November 2011-2014, as Member Secretary of the National Manufacturing Competitiveness Council (NMCC).

As Joint Secretary and then Additional Secretary in the Ministry of Power he played a key role in enactment of the Electricity Act, 2003, and Rules and policies under it.

As CEO, Greater NOIDA Industrial Development Authority, he was responsible for the development of one of the most attractive Industrial townships and attracting considerable FDI to it.

He was Secretary to the Lt. Governor of Delhi for over 5 years.

Before serving as Secretary (DIPP), he was Principal Adviser in the Planning Commission looking after Environment and Forests, Water and Sanitation as well as provision of Rural Infrastructure.

He has been a public policy scholar at the Woodrow Wilson Centre in Washington DC, USA. He has served on the Boards of major public sector companies and also as an Independent Director on the Boards of HAL and Tata Global Beverages.

He has a Masters in Political Science from Allahabad University and a Masters in Economics from Georgetown University, Washington DC.

CHANDRAJIT BANERJEE
Director General, CII

Chandrajit Banerjee is the Director General of the Confederation of Indian Industry (CII). Banerjee has been with the CII for about 3 decades and has been the Director General, CII since May 2008.

Banerjee is a Post-Graduate (MS) in Economics with specialisation on Economics of Planning and Econometrics from the University of Calcutta. Earlier, he did his Graduation from St. Xavier's College (Calcutta) in Economics (Hons).

As Director General, he is responsible for overall operations of CII. Over the years, Banerjee has worked out of the CII-Headquarters in New Delhi for several years and has also been based at Kolkata, Chennai, Mumbai, Chandigarh and Ahmedabad. He was also in Bangalore to initiate the Centre of Excellence of the Indian Machine

Tool Manufacturers' Association (IMTMA), which is a state-of-the-art centre for training, conventions and trade fairs.

He is an advisory Board Member of the Commonwealth Enterprise and Investment Council (CWEIC) and Member of Board of the Global Innovation and Technology Alliance (GITA). Banerjee is a Director in the Singapore India Partnership Foundation (SIPF), the Managing Trustee of the National Foundation for Corporate Governance (NFCG) and a Director at the Invest India.

Banerjee has been honored with the *China-India Friendship* Award by the Chinese Premier Wen Jiabao for his contributions towards the development of bilateral ties between India and China. Banerjee has also been conferred with the decoration of *Knight Commander of the Order of Queen Isabella* by His Majesty the King of Spain in recognition of his most meritorious achievements and exceptional contributions towards promoting relations between India and Spain.

LT GEN SATISH NAMBIAR (RETD)

Served in the Indian Army for 39 years and retired as the Deputy Chief on 31 August 1994. First Force Commander and Head of Mission of the UN forces in the former Yugoslavia—3 March 1992 to 2 March 1993. Adviser to the Govt. of Sri Lanka on peace process in 2001-02. Member UN High Level Panel on "Threats, Challenges and Change" 2003-04. Member International Advisory Board 'Security Council Report.' Chairman Advisory Board UNITAR PTP. Member International Verification Commission monitoring cease-fire declaration of ETA. Recipient of the VIR CHAKRA for bravery in battle, and PVSM and AVSM for distinguished service. Conferred the Padma Bhushan on Republic Day 2009 for contributions to national security affairs.

BRIGADIER GURMEET KANWAL (RETD)

Brigadier Gurmeet Kanwal (Retd) is Distinguished Fellow, Institute for Defence Studies and Analyses (IDSA), New Delhi and Adjunct Fellow, Centre for Strategic and International Studies (CSIS), Washington, D. C. He is former Director, Centre for Land Warfare

Studies (CLAWS), New Delhi (January 2008-March 2012). He has co-founded two Delhi-based think tanks: Forum for Strategic Initiatives (FSI) and the South Asian Institute for Strategic Affairs (SAISA).

Brig. Kanwal commanded an infantry brigade in the high-altitude Gurez Sector on the LoC with Pakistan in northern Kashmir (Operation Parakram, 2001-03) and an artillery regiment in counter-insurgency operations in Kashmir Valley (Operation Rakshak, 1993-94). He has served as United Nations Military Observer in UNTAG, Namibia; Brigade Major of an infantry brigade and Instructor-in-Gunnery at the School of Artillery, Devlali.

He was a Senior Fellow at the ORF and the Institute for Defence Studies and Analyses (IDSA) and the Centre for Air Power Studies, New Delhi. He has been a Visiting Research Scholar at the Cooperative Monitoring Centre (CMC), Sandia National Laboratories, Albuquerque, USA, and in other think tanks in London and Singapore.

Brigadier Kanwal has authored: *Nuclear Defence: Shaping the Arsenal*; *Indian Army: Vision 2020*; *Pakistan's Proxy War*; *Heroes of Kargil*; *Kargil' 99: Blood, Guts and Firepower,* and *Artillery: Honour and Glory* and edited several books.

In November 2012, he was included among 50 Thought Leaders in India by Mail Today.

PROF. CHINTAMANI MAHAPATRA

Prof. Chintamani Mahapatra is currently Rector (Pro-Vice Chancellor) of Jawaharlal Nehru University and Professor of American Studies at the School of International Studies of JNU.

He is also the Editor of Indian Foreign Affairs Journal.

He has held positions, such as Member, UGC Review Committee, Area Studies Programme, Member, Fellowship Expert Committee, ICSSR, Editor, Indian Foreign Affairs Journal, Member, Editorial Board, Strategic Analysis, IDSA, Member, Editorial Board, Diaspora Studies and Member, Committee on Studies, Academy of International Studies, Jamia Millia Islamia.

Recently, he was Tagore Chair Professor at Yunnan University of China. He has conducted research in several US Presidential Libraries and US National Archives; British Public Record Office in London.

Prof. Mahapatra has authored four books, three edited volumes, and has contributed chapters to above 30 edited books. He has published above 70 research articles in reputed journals.

He has been awarded a number of international fellowships, such as Fulbright Fellowship, Commonwealth Fellowship, and Visiting Fellowships to undertake research in the US, UK, Austria, Australia and many other countries.

LYDIA POWELL

Ms Lydia Powell has been with the Observer Research Foundation for over 18 years working on policy issues in energy, water and the environment in the Indian context. Her current interests include energy security, energy access, carbon constraints, clean coal and natural gas for energy and environmental security and federalism and its impact on Indian energy policy. She contributes commentary and analysis on the Indian energy sector regularly. Her most recent paper was a book chapter on India's Energy Transitions. Ms Powell has also worked for Norsk Hydro and for Orkla, two of Norway's largest conglomerates whose interests include energy. Ms. Powell has three Post Graduate Degrees—two on Energy from Norway and one in Solid State Physics from India.